BUSES

YEARBOOK 2009

Edited by STEWART J. BROWN

Ian Allan
PUBLISHING

BUSES
YEARBOOK 2009

Contents

First published 2008

ISBN 978 0 7110 3295 8

© Ian Allan Publishing Ltd 2008

Published by Ian Allan Publishing

an imprint of Ian Allan Publishing Ltd, Hersham, Surrey, KT12 4RG. Printed in England by Ian Allan Printing Ltd, Hersham, Surrey, KT12 4RG.

Code: 0808/E1

Visit the Ian Allan Publishing website at www.ianallanpublishing.com

Front cover: An East Lancs Cityzen-bodied Scania N113 in service with Brighton & Hove, the biggest single customer for this exclusive body/chassis combination. *Alan Millar*

Back cover (upper): Bristol is one of a number of cities investing in bus-priority schemes, among them this bus lane, being used by a Wessex Connect Volvo B7RLE/ Plaxton Centro on a park-and-ride service. *Stewart J. Brown*

Back cover (lower): Seen in Kowloon, Hong Kong, this Scania N113/Alexander was the first of two prototypes bought by KMB in 1993 to trial 'cleaner' engines. *Peter Rowlands*

Previous page: Go North East continues to specify route branding for its operations on Tyneside. This is a Mercedes-Benz Citaro in all-over gold for recently-introduced 'Citylink' route 58. *Stewart J. Brown*

Scania — four decades in Great Britain

It is 40 years since Scania first supplied Britain with buses. Here **Alan Millar**, Editor of *Buses* magazine, looks at the company's development over four decades in this country.

Scania ended 2007 supplying just over 11% of all new buses and coaches delivered to UK operators. That made it the fourth-largest supplier, after Volvo, Alexander Dennis and Optare. If you prefer numbers to percentages, that was 452 vehicles for a range of customers large and small, including National Express, Stagecoach, Go-Ahead Group, Metroline, Lothian Buses, Nottingham City Transport, Ipswich Buses and Newport Transport.

Lest you think this was some kind of record for the Swedish giant — one of the five biggest European bus manufacturers — it wasn't. A series of possibly temporary setbacks saw it do worse than the year before, when 547 sales gave it almost 13% of the UK market, 100 vehicles ahead of Optare. In 2006 nearly a quarter of Scania buses and coaches delivered in Western Europe went to UK operators, and nearly one in 10 of its worldwide sales were in the UK. Having set itself a target of increasing worldwide bus and coach sales from 6,000 to 10,000 units within the next few years, the company expects to build on its past successes and could conceivably sell around 900 vehicles a year in the UK — closer to the sales currently accomplished by Volvo and Alexander Dennis.

Its achievement is all the more remarkable when you consider three key facts. It has done it by organic growth, gaining market share by selling and supporting its products, and not by acquiring an established UK business. Its model range is relatively limited, with nothing light enough to give it a credible presence in the largest market segment, for midibuses. And its initial presence in the UK wasn't covered in unalloyed glory.

That initial presence began in 1969, 40 years before the date on this *Yearbook* cover, and marked the beginning of an initially slow, yet radical transformation of the UK bus market. Imports of foreign-built coaches had ended with the outbreak of World War 2 in September 1939 and were only beginning to get underway again with small numbers of Mercedes-Benz O302s from Germany and Caetano-bodied British chassis from Portugal.

Above: A Scania N94UD/East Lancs OmniDekka in Go-Ahead's Brighton & Hove fleet.

Bus imports ended with the consolidation of the operating industry from 1930 and the rise — and rapidly improving quality — of larger vehicles produced in particular by Leyland, AEC and Bedford. With large parts of the operating industry in state or local-authority ownership, and buying British being the aspiration of the private sector, there was a lot of resistance to the idea of purchasing imported vehicles. On top of that, import duties had long added to their cost.

By 1969 many of the old certainties were changing — not least in the degree of real choice available to UK operators. In the 20 years after World War 2 ended in 1945 the manufacturing industry was consolidated through a series of mergers and acquisitions, culminating with the creation in 1968 of British Leyland out of the Leyland Motor Corporation and British Motor Holdings. In the bus market, LMC owned Leyland, AEC and Albion and had an influential 25% shareholding in Bristol, as well as owning Park Royal and Charles Roe in the body market, along with 25% of Eastern Coach Works. BMH owned Daimler and Guy. The only home-market chassis manufacturers outside the new grouping were American-owned Ford and Bedford, which were strongest in the coach sector

3

and offered only lightweight single-deckers in the bus market, and Seddon, which would soon also pass into American ownership and was a small player in coaches and buses.

This restructure also created uncertainty among independent bodybuilders, as British Leyland had the capability — and desire — to build complete integral-construction vehicles, starting with the Leyland National single-decker. That threat was felt most keenly by Metro-Cammell Weymann, which had enjoyed a 20-year partnership with Leyland, starting with the Olympic integral single-decker and continuing with a hand-in-glove relationship that saw MCW body most early Atlantean double-deckers.

MCW explored possible tie-ups with Ford and Bedford, which at the time were developing heavy-duty truck chassis, but it was with Scania (or Scania-Vabis, as it was still called) that it agreed a deal to build a vehicle to compete with the Leyland National in what then seemed to be the most promising market sector. Many operators were replacing crew-operated double-deckers with one-person-operated single-deckers, but double-deckers were fast coming back into vogue when the prototype Metro-Scanias appeared in 1969.

Scania's citybus range had an intriguing international pedigree. Although built in Sweden primarily for its home market, the transverse rear-engined vehicles had developed out of a Mack design built in the United States and which Scania had manufactured under licence in 1953/4. From the mid-1950s Scania fitted its own 11.1-litre D11 engine, developed from the Leyland O.680, to which it had also obtained licensing rights. From the outset these vehicles had fully automatic torque-converter transmission, at a time when their British counterparts had semi-automatic at best, and by the mid-1960s the comparison was even starker. Scania fitted air suspension when most British buses had leaf springs; power steering was standard yet a rarity in Britain, and turbocharging and other technical advances made the engines more powerful, quieter and cleaner than the likes of the O.680 from which they had sprung.

Sweden caught up with the rest of mainland Europe in 1967 by switching to driving on the right. Although many mid-life right-hand-drive buses were rebuilt, the boom in demand created an opportunity for Leyland to sell 250 left-hand-drive Park Royal-bodied Panthers and Atlanteans to Stockholm, but the British manufacturer failed to sustain that success. There was no repeat order. The increase in demand created capacity that Scania was happy to fill subsequently with new export business, and the UK tie-up with MCW came at the right time, especially as Scania was also beginning to sell trucks in the UK.

Sweden's move to driving on the right nearly took Scania into one corner of the UK in 1967. Ulsterbus, newly formed to take over the Ulster Transport Authority's buses, wanted to replace the AEC Reliances on its Derry City services and tried out an ex-Stockholm Scania-Vabis Capitol C70 dating from around 1955. It looked like a tank and had an unladen weight to match, resulting in fuel consumption practically twice that of the buses it would have replaced. With Ulsterbus striving to operate without any public subsidy, this was an offer easily refused.

The Metro-Scania was more acceptable. It was based on Scania's CR110 integral (which from 1966 to 1968 had been called the CR76) and used light alloy panelling to keep its weight down. The UK bus had the substantially similar BR110 chassis modules and Scania's own Swedish body design altered at the front and rear to accommodate a larger back window and a signature asymmetric windscreen (deeper on the nearside to provide extra kerbside visibility) designed by MCW. The first vehicles were built entirely in Sweden, production at Birmingham beginning in 1971.

By now the apparent trend towards large-scale single-deck operation had passed, partly through operators' dissatisfaction with most of the chassis developed by the constituent parts of British Leyland, and the Leyland National satisfied much of what demand did exist. Even so, this virtually unknown newcomer followed its two prototypes with orders for 131. Its first major customer was Leicester City Transport, which was swimming hard against national trends by trying to use higher-quality buses to entice motorists out of their cars, and took 35. Newport Corporation, which was equally innovative in accelerating its fleet renewal to eliminate conductor operation, became the model's biggest customer, with an order for 44.

The other 52 were spread more widely around England and Wales. Three PTEs — Merseyside, SELNEC and West Midlands — took 34 between them, London Transport six, and London Country four (for Stevenage SuperBus services), to which it added the only examples sold to an independent, these being the three inherited by the National Bus Company when Hants & Dorset took over King Alfred of Winchester. South Wales municipals Taff Ely (Pontypridd) and Merthyr Tydfil took three and two respectively.

These sales proved that there clearly was interest, perhaps demand, for buses produced by someone other than Leyland, and that some sales could be sustained. But with such a modest requirement for single-deckers the Metro-Scania was transformed into a double-decker. In 1972 MCW and Scania confirmed that one was in development, and this emerged the following year as the Metropolitan.

Above: A Leicester Metro-Scania demonstrating its then class-beating low engine-noise levels. *Author's collection*

While the Metro-Scania was offered in 10.3m and 11m lengths there was just one — shorter — length of Metropolitan to suit a market dominated by 9.5m vehicles. Its BR111 running units were similar to those of the single-decker, albeit with its two radiators moved ahead of the rear axle. The body was more British in style, derived from MCW's standard body on Leyland chassis but with the asymmetric windscreen and metal body trim carried over from the single-decker.

Like the single-decker it was in a league apart from the competition, which still featured naturally aspirated engines, epicyclic gearboxes, leaf suspension and relatively slow acceleration. It was announced in the same week that Volvo's importer unveiled the other challenger for double-deck orders, the British-designed and -built Ailsa, with a tiny turbocharged engine on the front platform. Both designs met operators' demands for a more acceptable double-decker at a time when Leyland's Atlantean, Daimler Fleetline and Bristol VRT all had perceived weaknesses. While the Ailsa met this with simplicity and ruggedness, the Metropolitan offered sophistication and advanced engineering.

MCW's sales efforts also ensured that its model enjoyed greater initial success, two prototypes being followed by 661 built between the springs of 1974 and 1978, years when demand for new buses was stoked up by the availability of 50% capital grants from central government. Most went to big cities. London Transport — deeply frustrated by its problems with Fleetlines — placed the largest single order, for 164. Six of the

seven PTEs (all except West Midlands) between them took 349, of which Tyne & Wear accounted for 140 and West Yorkshire 95.

Four municipals took 141 between them, Leicester building on its earlier satisfaction with the Metro-Scania to take 68 and Newport, which had little need of many more new buses, buying 10. Reading took 33 and Hull 30, both later adding secondhand examples from Merseyside PTE and London Transport respectively. The National Bus Company bought five for Maidstone & District, for comparative trials against five Ailsas and some Bristol VRTs, while in 1975 two were exported, to China Motor Bus in Hong Kong.

The customer base may not have been broad, but this was still remarkable for a chassis type with no prior British pedigree, competing in a market where public undertakings risked criticism for buying perceptibly foreign products. And it was impressive as some customers — notably Tyne & Wear, Leicester and Reading — placed repeat orders. So did other PTEs, but generally before their first examples entered service.

Like the single-decker, the Metropolitan impressed on first encounter, being nippier, quieter and smoother-running than its British peers and predecessors. But there were longer-term problems. Fuel consumption was high, and these buses arrived on the market as Middle East turmoil triggered big rises in the price of crude oil. The two-speed Scania gearbox also proved less reliable here than in Sweden, a problem that exposed the high cost of replacement parts. Later it became clear that placing unprotected steel and aluminium components in close proximity rendered the bus prone to serious corrosion problems. Added to

that, in inadequately trained hands the lively performance of this most easily driven bus led to some skidding accidents.

Some operators gave up soon after these difficulties became apparent. London Transport, which had great difficulty adapting to the post-Routemaster age and had already condemned to premature disposal more than 4,000 single- and double-deckers dating from the mid-1960s to the mid-1970s, started retiring its Metropolitans, having already also sold its surplus Metro-Scanias to Newport, while Merseyside, Greater Glasgow and West Yorkshire PTEs also withdrew theirs prematurely.

In the meantime Dennis had been persuaded to develop the Dominator double-decker with Gardner engine and Voith gearbox, and Northern Counties had worked with Foden on prototypes of a similar bus with Allison transmission. However, it was MCW that effectively sealed the Metropolitan's fate by developing its own Metrobus chassis with similar driveline to that of the Dennis. Scania's fortunes were not helped by a change of general manager at Leicester, as new appointee Geoffrey Hilditch encouraged Dennis in its endeavours and made the industry aware of his dissatisfaction with the fuel consumption of his Metropolitans. The Metrobus first saw the light of day in 1978, and the agreement with Scania was formally terminated the following year, when the Swedish manufacturer assumed responsibility for parts and service for the vehicles already built.

As if things weren't bad enough for Scania, the market for new buses was about to contract dramatically. New Bus Grant, introduced in 1968 as a 12-year measure to hasten the conversion to one-person operation, was extended beyond 1980, but only to cushion the blow for manufacturers. Over the next four years it was reduced from 40% to 10%, and operators — which had already taken advantage of the 50% grant to buy more vehicles than normal — took maximum advantage of the remaining grant. Suddenly too many factories — and almost certainly too many manufacturers — were chasing a diminishing volume of business. Yet this was when Scania began to compete in the UK market in its own right.

Not only did it reveal plans for a new BR112DH double-deck chassis to succeed the Metropolitan, but at the model's UK launch in 1980 Scania was also brave (or foolhardy) enough to tell the bus press how many it hoped to sell: 200 a year. Metropolitan sales — in a market desperate for buses — had averaged 166 a year, so this was optimism in the extreme. Over the next eight years it sold just 117 in the UK, of which 45 — nine of them single-deckers — went to one customer, Newport, which proved that at least one of the Metro-Scania's conquests had turned into a loyal customer.

The BR112DH, re-designated N112 in 1984, had a proper chassis frame, a single offside radiator, the option of either a three-speed Scania or a Voith automatic gearbox and a choice of 9.5m and 10.2m lengths. It also had a wide choice of bodywork, with double-deckers by East Lancs, Marshall, Alexander and Northern Counties; Newport's single-deckers had Wadham Stringer bodies.

It says much for operators' patriotism and British manufacturers' lobbying strength with the public sector that Scania came off so badly in this struggle, missing out even when orders were split between manufacturers. Leyland continued to dominate the market with its new Olympian and Titan (and even the aged Atlantean in Manchester and Liverpool), while the MCW Metrobus did well in London and the West Midlands. Dennis and Volvo, the latter building the Ailsa and later the B10M-derived Citybus in Scotland, took up most remaining demand.

However, to lapse into the clichéed world of football, this was a game of two halves. In the last years of the old regulated, largely state-owned bus industry sales beyond Newport were limited mostly to trial purchases, like an Alexander-bodied pair for Tyne & Wear PTE and a Northern Counties-bodied pair for Greater Manchester. By contrast, deregulation, privatisation and the introduction of tendering in London broke past purchasing allegiances, especially as Scania (and other manufacturers) built buses for stock so that operators could take delivery at short notice.

Of 81 N112s built for the UK only 16 went to Newport. The largest single batch was of 23 Van Hool-bodied single-deckers for shuttle work at Heathrow Airport, but there were significant sales for conventional bus work. Grey-Green, the original bus and coach company in what later became Arriva, bought six East Lancs-bodied double-deckers for London tendered work, Hull (one of the Metropolitan's more satisfied customers) took six East Lancs-bodied single-deckers, and Brighton & Hove, breaking free of its National Bus Company past, took 10 East Lancs-bodied double-deckers. This was a turning-point, the building-block on which Scania steadily increased its UK market share — a process helped by the demise of MCW, which built its last Metrobuses in 1989.

By this time Scania had broadened its product range

for the UK to take it into the coach market and give it an alternative offering for bus operators. This was the K-series, introduced here in 1982, with deliveries starting in 1983. It had a vertical rear engine mounted in-line with the chassis rather than transversely, as on the N-series. As a result the driveline was simpler and more fuel-efficient. In 1981 Scania had built two right-hand-drive Jonckheere-bodied BR116 coaches — similar to the new 11-litre K112, but the preceding model — to raise operator awareness. MCW had earlier (in 1973) imported a solitary Scania-bodied, V8-engined CR145 coach for trials on the National Express network, but that project was not pursued.

In the new model's first two years Scania sold an impressive 69 K112s, most with Jonckheere bodies, although Van Hool and Plaxton bodied a few; a Plaxton-bodied demonstrator was sold to PMT, making it the first NBC company to buy a Scania since the Maidstone & District Metropolitans. From 1985 the K112 was joined by the K92, of similar layout but with an 8.5-litre engine; although this provided Scania with a lighter and less powerful coach it sold better as a bus, with Jonckheere, East Lancs and Alexander bodywork. Most were single-deckers; there were two pairs of high-capacity 11m East Lancs-bodied double-deckers — for Maidstone Boro'line and Grey-Green — but no more were built.

When production ended in 1988 Scania had sold 339 K92s and K112s in the UK. This was part of Scania's Series 2 family, a wider range of buses, coaches and trucks, which was now succeeded by the Series 3, with cleaner and more powerful engines and improved braking and suspension. Initially the new bus and coach range built on what had gone before

Above left: The biggest user of the Metropolitan outside London was the Tyne & Wear PTE, which had 140. This 1977 example is seen in central Newcastle when just a few months old. *Stewart J. Brown*

Right: Still in service as a school bus nearly 20 years after it was built, this is one of the high-capacity East Lancs-bodied K92 double-deckers new to Boro'line Maidstone. *Daniel Stazicker*

— N113 and K93 buses, K93 and K113 coaches. The change coincided with a change of selling arrangements, Scania transferring customer contact from its UK head office in Milton Keynes to two dealers — Worksop-based Stuart Johnson (latterly the MCW dealer) covering England and Wales, and Reliable Vehicles similarly in Scotland; although these were independent businesses in 1989, both dealers would later pass into Scania ownership.

Bus sales accelerated, especially with the N113. Repeat business was evident with Brighton & Hove buying 20 double-deckers by 1990 and another 31 by 1998; Hull took 16, while by 1994 Nottingham had bought 16 new, along with 10 secondhand N112s

and N113s (three of them former demonstrators).

There also were important new customers. The former PTE undertakings, not yet part of major groups, were beginning to buy substantial numbers of new buses. Whilst continuing to favour Leyland, Busways, the former Tyne & Wear fleet (and, prior to deregulation, one of the few buyers of the BR112), took 10 double-deckers and 38 single-deckers, including an ex-demonstrator and a three-year-old bus new to Stevensons of Uttoxeter. Yorkshire Rider, the former West Yorkshire undertaking, bought 42 double-deckers and 55 single-deckers. West Midlands Travel, whose PTE predecessor had operated only a solitary Metro-Scania single-decker, took 40 double-deckers.

Left: Plaxton bodied Scania coaches until the early 1990s. This is a Paramount 3500-bodied K113 new to Yorkshire Traction, which company's colours it retained with a subsequent operator in the Scottish Borders.
Phil Halewood

Right: One of the Alexander RH-bodied N113 double-deckers bought by Yorkshire Rider between privatisation and sale to Badgerline.
Phil Halewood

And London Buses bought 71 double-deckers between 1989 and 1992, a period when it spread its ordering favours quite widely.

Yorkshire Traction, which had several Scania coaches, was another ex-NBC operator to turn its back on past diktat. It liked buying buses in batches of five, following five Alexander-bodied N113 single-deckers in 1991 with 10 Wright Endurance-bodied K93s in 1992/3. Another highly significant order came from GRT Holdings — precursor of FirstGroup — for 26 Wright Endurance-bodied N113s, which were delivered in 1994/5.

By 1993 Scania's UK sales were tailing off again, down from 211 and a market share of 8% in 1990 to end the year with only 121 registrations and 5.3% of the market. This was as far as sales declined, for three important additions were made to the range that year.

For coach customers it entered into an exclusive arrangement to import the Spanish-built Irizar Century body on two- and three-axle K113 chassis, offering a highly specified standard product at an attractive price. Although, in its home market, Irizar also fitted this body on Volvo, Mercedes-Benz, MAN and Iveco chassis, only Scania sold it in the UK, and its visual appeal helped win customers who might not otherwise have considered a K113. Scania has since developed its relationship with Irizar across many world markets and regards the Spanish coachbuilder as a key bodybuilding partner.

Of the two additional buses, one was more significant for the trend it represented than for the model itself. This was the low-floor (or, strictly, low-entry) version of the N113 single-decker. Low-floor buses were becoming increasingly common in mainland Europe, notably Germany and Scandinavia, and London Transport was sponsoring the biggest UK trial with an order for 68. All were bodied by Wright, 38 on Dennis Lance SLF, the other 30 on the low-floor

N113. For sales beyond London Scania also offered the MaxCi, the same chassis units in an East Lancs-built body based on a Scania body built for Scandinavia. A demonstrator and a solitary example for Tayside were followed by nine stock vehicles sold to British Bus companies (since absorbed by Arriva) and a further demonstrator that ended up with Yorkshire Rider. These 42 low-floor N113s were the only ones built for the UK, but Newport continued to take small batches of step-entrance Alexander Strider-bodied N113s until 1997.

The demise of the N113 single-decker is partly explained by the success of the other addition announced in 1993, the L113. This chassis, developed in 1989 as a city bus for South America and also sold

Left: The first low-floor Scania bus for the UK, an East Lancs-bodied N113 MaxCi, for Tayside. *Scania*

Below: First fleets bought nearly 250 examples of the L113/Wright Axcess-ultralow. This one was operating newly acquired ChesterBus routes in 2007. *Mark Haldon*

as an inter-urban bus in Scandinavia, was a cross between the N113 and K113. The front section of the chassis was of similar height to the N113 but with a beam axle, while the in-line engine was inclined to the side to reduce the floor height at the back. It was cheaper to buy and used less fuel than the N113, and had a more acceptable back end than the K113. It also had better weight distribution than the N113, which was near the limit over the back axle.

The first deliveries of L113s had step-entrance bodies by Alexander, Northern Counties and East Lancs, but the new model came into its own from 1995 with a low-floor Wright body. At the time this 47-seater — marketed jointly as the Axcess-ultralow — was the highest capacity 12m low-floor single-decker in the UK. It also was better laid-out inside, with a less obvious

difference in height between the front and rear sections. By far its biggest customer was FirstBus/Group, which was growing rapidly and placing large orders for new vehicles. More than 300 (including nearly 250 for First) were supplied before the model was replaced in 1998.

In 1997, to comply with Euro3 emission limits, Scania introduced its 4-series buses and trucks. The big change in the bus and coach range was to replace the 11-litre engine in its urban buses with a new 9-litre unit, so the L113 gave way to the L94, which for the UK was offered in three forms — the 12m low-floor L94UB, articulated L94UA and inter-urban L94IB, which extended the coach range to include a lower-height Irizar body, the Intercentury. The Wright-bodied low-floor bus initially became the Axcess Floline, and, after the bodybuilder's replacement Millennium range went into production in 2000, this version of the body was replaced by the Solar.

Again, First was initially the biggest customer, taking more than 350, although quantities tailed off as the group placed the greatest proportion of its orders with Volvo and supplemented these with small orders for Scanias. This contrasted with the situation elsewhere, as Volvo's primary Euro3 chassis was the B7L, with a vertical engine in the nearside rear; this layout was fine for left-hand-drive buses with three doors on the (British) offside, but it created an awkward layout on typical single-door right-hand-drive UK buses. Several hitherto satisfied Volvo customers — notably Go North East, and Translink in Northern Ireland — switched to the L94. Another notable convert was Trent Barton, which had previously favoured Optare.

Scania replaced the N113 with the 9-litre-engined N94, but this wasn't available initially in the UK. And, having peaked with 323 bus and coach registrations

Right: Wright Solar-bodied Scanias are operated by MK Metro, now a subsidiary of Arriva. *Stewart J. Brown*

Left: Translink turned to the Wright Solar-bodied L94 following unhappy experience with the Volvo B7L. This one is in the Ulsterbus fleet; others are with Metro in Belfast.

in 1998 and achieved a creditable 289 in 1999, sales dropped to 191 in 2000 and 178 in 2001, Scania's worst performance in seven years. The big gap in the range was a double-decker; not only was the N113 no longer available, but it lacked a low-floor version at a time when Volvo, DAF and Dennis offered such double-deckers. Three loyal customers — Nottingham, Brighton & Hove and Newport — all bought Dennis Tridents, though Scania would subsequently win all of them back.

In the meantime Scania displayed some ingenuity in disposing of its last N113s, which by 1998/9 were not what core-market bus buyers wanted. In 1995 it had teamed up with East Lancs to offer a unique body, the Cityzen, on this chassis, selling 50 in all — 31 to Brighton & Hove, 13 to British Bus-owned Northumbria and six to Mayne's of Manchester, which had become a regular Scania customer. Following a one-off order for a similar bus for Fowler's of Holbeach Drove it had another 35 built, some with bus seats and others with coach seats fitted with seatbelts, selling two more to Mayne's and the remainder to 17 small- to medium-sized operators, primarily for the private-hire market for school parties. Most of these operators would

otherwise have bought second-hand vehicles.

The N94 was finally introduced to the UK at the beginning of 2002 and marked a highly important turning-point, for it was at this time that Scania started offering its own bodywork to UK customers. It had been selling complete bodied buses and coaches in left-hand-drive markets for a long time and since 1996 had packaged the N series within its integral OmniCity, a full low-floor single-decker designed to be an attractive feature of city streets.

It hired the services of Leyland Product Developments, a Lancashire business hived off by Volvo, to develop a right-hand-drive OmniCity. LPD produced a prototype, the first of 44 supplied to Nottingham City Transport by 2007. Initially buses for the UK were built in Sweden, but in 2004 production transferred to its plant at Słupsk, across the Baltic in Poland.

Scania's most loyal UK customer, Newport, standardised on the OmniCity, and other notable deliveries were to Go-Ahead-owned Metrobus and Go North East, First (37 for its Hampshire & Dorset and Potteries fleets in 2004-6), Ipswich Buses and Reading Transport, as well as several smaller

Left: An East Lancs Cityzen-bodied N113 in service with Astons of Kempsey, one of a number of operators to avail themselves of the opprtunity to acquire new double-deckers.

Above right: All of the major groups — Arriva, National Express, First, Go-Ahead and Stagecoach — operate vehicles from Scania's Polish-built Omni range. This is an Arriva OmniCity in Gateshead.
Stewart J. Brown

operators. Cardiff Bus, First Manchester and Travel West Midlands all took articulated versions, but Scania's hopes of sharing some of Mercedes-Benz's success in supplying artics to London came to nothing. Two other versions of the N94 were developed in collaboration with East Lancs. The more successful was the OmniDekka, Scania's low-floor UK double-decker, which became available from early 2003. This was offered in two lengths, 10.7m and 11.9m, with a restyled version of the body East Lancs also built on Volvo, DAF and Dennis chassis; the most obvious change was to incorporate an OmniCity windscreen and lower dash in place of either of the bodybuilder's own choice of two designs.

Scania's unique sales proposition was to offer the OmniDekka with more lower-deck seating than any of its competitors of equal length — especially attractive in London, where centre exit doors, straight staircases and wheelchair bays left low-floor double-deckers with fewer seats than their step-entrance predecessors.

A further unique selling point was that, because of its fully low-floor chassis, it could be built to a lower overall height, which enabled it to comply with Transport for London's minimum upper-deck ceiling height of 1.8m (6ft 1in) within an overall height of 4.21m (13ft 9¾in). In theory this also was good news for London operators, especially big groups, as they could cascade mid-life OmniDekkas to other parts of the country without worrying about them being too tall to fit into low-doored garages or under low bridges. This was a genuine concern. For a time Stagecoach had persuaded the London tendering people to let it

buy lowheight Olympians for services in the capital on the understanding that its tender prices would be lower if it knew they could be cascaded elsewhere. And Arriva asked East Lancs to develop a conversion package to allow it to detach high London roofs and replace them with lower ones when buses were to be cascaded. It did not pursue the idea, nor did it buy the OmniDekka.

One problem with these theories was that the extra seats in the OmniDekka were squeezed in behind the back axle, and the low ceilings on the lower deck meant that passengers could easily bang their heads getting in and out. By the end of 2006 TfL had redrawn its specifications to require more headroom downstairs and East Lancs had to produce a taller version.

Even so, Scania had a double-decker it could sell in London and elsewhere. For London, Metrobus amassed a total of 110, while Transdev took 64. Brighton & Hove reverted to its preferred double-deck supplier, taking 108 OmniDekkas, while by the end of 2007 Nottingham had 80, and Reading 34. First took 30 in 2004/5, and by December 2005 Stagecoach, which had yet to order any new Scanias (although it had inherited many through takeovers) had 12 OmniDekkas — five operated in Corby on behalf of Northamptonshire County Council and seven acquired with Yorkshire Traction.

Nottingham, Reading and Brighton & Hove bought examples of the 11.9m version, which had up to 90 seats, although a similar bus built for evaluation by Lothian Buses was returned after it was discovered to exceed the legal weight limit.

The less popular of the East Lancs collaborations was the OmniTown, based on the 10.7m single-deck N94. It was a product of two desires on Scania's part: to offer a small bus to compete with the Dennis Dart and other midibuses, and not to upset Wrightbus, its long-term single-deck body partner. Compared with the Dart and its closest competitors the OmniTown was heavier and had larger wheels and fewer seats, but Scania argued that it was more durable and would cost less over its lifetime. And, as there was no equivalent Scania/Wright product, it appealed to a different market sector from the L94.

The OmniTown, with Scania front, was ordered by Nottingham, which took seven for tram-feeder services, and OFJ Connections of Staines, which took four for transfer work around Heathrow Airport. These vehicles followed an initial production run with East Lancs's existing Myllennium-style front, of which 14 ordered by Durham Travel Services went to TfL-owned East Thames Buses after DTS collapsed, while another (plus the demonstrator) went to Mayne's of Manchester. Later, in 2006, Metrobus took 23 with East Lancs' Esteem-style front for TfL routes, and similar vehicles followed for Thames Travel of Wallingford and Centrebus of Leicester, but Scania's sales story did not defeat the Dart and its ilk.

Before any were built, Scania had toyed with having the OmniTown bodied in Spain by Castrosua and had a prototype built, which eventually was sold to The King's Ferry and used to transport asylum seekers between Cambridge and temporary accommodation in a nearby detention centre.

Left: An Irizar PB-bodied K-series at the UK Coach Rally in Brighton.

Above right: Lothian has 15 Euro3 OmniCity double-deckers for its Edinburgh Airport service. *Keith McGillivray*

Below: A Caetano Levante-bodied K340 of Arriva Midlands operating a National Express service through Evesham.

For Euro3, Scania's main coach product was the K114, sold increasingly with the Irizar Century body, supplemented at the top end by the 12-litre K124 and at the bottom end by the L94, which was also used as the basis of the S-Kool, a school-bus version of the Intercentury.

For 2003 the range was expanded with the K124-based Irizar PB, a new high-floor body with sloping pillars that had the by-product of giving the rear window the backward-raked appearance of the 1959 Ford Anglia car. The Century body was facelifted in 2004, and in 2007 the Intercentury was replaced by the Irizar i4, part of a new range with Euro4 engines.

The modern appearance of the PB appealed to National Express, which specified it for its own fleet and those of some of its contractors as part of a drive to broaden the appeal of its express coach services with features like leather seats. From 2006 NatEx standardised on the new wheelchair-accessible Caetano Levante body, initially on Scania and Volvo chassis, before announcing a three-year order for 120 three-axle Scanias on Euro4-engined K340 (replacement for the K114, the new numbers denoting horsepower rather than engine capacity and product series) for 2007-9. By then Scania was supplying most of its other UK coach business with Irizar bodies. The remainder was divided between Berkhof and Van Hool. It last took Plaxton bodies in 1991/2.

The near-overnight success of the OmniDekka convinced Scania that it could gain a bigger share of the UK market but also exposed a potential obstacle.

East Lancs had limited capacity at its Blackburn factory, and, for all its success in gaining new custom, some customers wanted more choice of bodywork. For a time it looked as if Wrightbus would develop the Solar Gemini, a version of the double-deck body built on Volvo and VDL (formerly DAF) chassis. But that came to nothing, partly because the bodybuilder was concerned about the unladen weight of the N94. Instead Scania produced a double-deck version of the OmniCity, to be built in Poland. Like the right-hand-drive single-decker, this was developed with help from Leyland Product Developments, which built one of the prototypes, and it became available in 2005. Initial production was limited, a prototype being supplied to Travel West Midlands, 15 going to Transdev in London, and 15 to Lothian for its Edinburgh Airport service. All were Euro3 models built to the lower height subsequently deemed unsuitable for London. The lack of a higher version also limited Lothian's interest, as it wanted more headroom on its normal city buses.

Scania — and German manufacturer MAN, which coincidentally has been trying to acquire or merge with Scania — took a different tack from the other major truck and bus manufacturers with the move to Euro4 and Euro5 engines, which became compulsory from October 2007. There are two main methods of cleaning up engines to achieve these lower emission limits. Most manufacturers chose selective catalytic reduction (SCR), which requires the addition of AdBlue fuel re-agent, while Scania and MAN went for exhaust-gas recirculation (EGR), which doesn't.

Several operators preferred EGR. Reading is one, Thamesdown — which opted to buy Scanias for the first time because of EGR — is another, and Stagecoach selected EGR for a substantial proportion of its vehicle intake from 2007 onwards, prompting it to order new Scanias for the UK for the first time in its 27-year existence.

The Euro4 engine range included a fundamental change, as a new five-cylinder 9-litre engine replaced the six-cylinder unit in the L94 and N94. And, in an economy measure, while the old engine was inclined on both models, the Euro4 was available only in upright format (spelling the end of the L-series).

Above: A Polish-built OmniCity of Go North East, with West Durham Swift branding.

Although more compact, it sat higher in the chassis — and required additional intercooling to make the EGR system work.

Scania also added another complete model with Polish bodywork. This was the OmniLink, the integral equivalent of the Wright Solar-bodied K-series and available with the additional option of a tri-axle 13.7m version with around 55 seats. The first three long

Below: One of Stagecoach's tri-axle 13.7m OmniLinks on a Fife-Edinburgh service.

examples went to Nottingham, which has since taken three 12m versions with ethanol engines, while Stagecoach took nine tri-axle vehicles for services between Edinburgh and Fife.

Stagecoach also further broadened Scania's double-deck offering by specifying 25 N230 double-deckers with Alexander Dennis Enviro400 bodies, reviving a body/chassis choice last available in the early 1990s. It is no coincidence that Stagecoach Chief Executive Brian Souter is one of the main shareholders in Alexander Dennis.

The broader body choice came at an appropriate time, as Scania's dependence on East Lancs threatened to undermine its growth plans during 2007. The bodybuilder began updating its product range the previous year, starting with its new Esteem single-decker. It built the first (a demonstrator since sold to Centrebus) on a Euro4 version of what had been called the OmniTown but now was just a 10.6m N230 and took orders from Preston Bus for eleven 12m versions.

The new double-deck body, the Olympus, was launched later the same year and became available on Scania chassis — as an alternative to the OmniDekka — with the switch to Euro4. A series of problems unfolded. The switch to Euro4 delayed chassis supply, the chassis were heavier (especially at the back), and, when completed, the dual-door London versions failed their tilt test and needed to lose seats (and weight).

These troubled vehicles were the last OmniDekkas for Metrobus (the first to the increased height), nine Olympuses for Transdev and 26 more for Metroline, which was buying its first Scanias as part of a move to maximise its use of EGR engines. Six single-door Olympus-bodied N230s for Reading were completed without any great difficulty.

Taken together, these problems proved to be the last straw for East Lancs, which was trading precariously, and the company went into administration. It was acquired almost instantly by a new company called Darwen Group, but the whole episode delayed many outstanding orders, including a batch of 13 Olympus-bodied Scanias for Cardiff — its first new double-deckers for about 15 years — and more buses for Reading. These problems help explain why 2007 wasn't Scania's best year in the UK.

At the time of writing (June 2008) Stagecoach had ordered a further 56 Enviro400-bodied Scanias, while the only significant order for East Lancs-bodied double-deckers was for 16 OmniDekkas for Nottingham. But Scania has secured several orders for the Polish-built double-decker — 14 with ethanol engines for Reading, 36 diesels for Go-Ahead fleets in Southern England and 38 for East London Bus Group, which placed its first order since being sold by Stagecoach. Scania also is developing hybrid diesel-electric buses for operation across Europe, vital if it is to win longer-term orders in London, especially as Alexander Dennis, Wrightbus and Optare are already making great strides in this direction.

Between 1990 and 2007 Scania supplied over 5,200 diesel buses and coaches in the UK. While it has not stated a date by which it expects to be selling 10,000 buses a year worldwide, the trend of the past 40 suggests that this is an objective it will gain with its steadily growing slice of the UK market.

Right: The future?
A prototype Scania hybrid bus for city operation.
Scania

Greyhound in print

The great days of the most famous name in world coaching were arguably the 20 years from the mid-1930s to the mid-1950s. **Stewart J. Brown** looks at printed ephemera which promoted the iconic American Greyhound business.

Greyhound is probably the most famous name in coaching, anywhere. The name was officially adopted in 1929, and today the operation is part of FirstGroup's significant North American business, having been acquired in 2007 as part of the group's expansion in the USA.

In the 1930s Greyhound Bus Lines was expanding and modernising. In 1936 it introduced rear-engined coaches — or should that be 'busses' in American parlance? — and also adopted fashionable art-deco styling for new terminals, or depots as they were often called.

It is a measure of the glamour of travel by Greyhound that its stylish terminals were the subject of equally stylish picture postcards in the 1930s and '40s. Would a postcard of the bus station in Leeds have the same cachet as one showing the Greyhound terminal in Louisville?

Greyhound ran high-profile advertising campaigns and issued postcards to promote its fleet and its services. Publicity material charts the development of the Greyhound fleet. Before 1935 it features normal-control coaches. From 1936 adverts and postcards show the new generation of 37-seat rear-engined integral coaches. These were built by Yellow Coach, initially with petrol engines and later with diesels.

A 1938 advert boasts that 'modern Super-Coaches are miracles of smooth riding – healthfully heated and ventilated'. Superlatives abounded. Another advert announces: 'No sleek, special-built limousine can exceed the riding ease of a Greyhound Super-Coach with its brilliantly designed body, extra long wheelbase — its four-position reclining chairs, efficient ventilation and heating.'

An updated version of the Super-Coach — dubbed the Silversides — was unveiled in 1940, but production ceased in 1941 because of World War 2, not restarting until 1947, at which time Greyhound ordered no fewer than 1,500, at a cost of $39 million. That was the largest single order in the company's history. By this time Yellow Coach had become the Truck & Coach Division of General Motors.

Greyhound featured in songs — most famously in the 1960s Chuck Berry ballad 'Promised Land'.

A study in 2007 by the DePaul University of Chicago says that between 1960 and 1980 scheduled coach services in the USA were reduced by one third, and that from 1980 to 2006 more than half of the remaining services were cut. But it ends optimistically, stating that since 2006 there has been a recovery, fuelled in part by investment by Greyhound and by the launch of new low-cost intercity services such as Stagecoach's Megabus.

Even if the great days of Greyhound are in the past, the company still provides a comprehensive low-cost network of services carrying 22 million people a year. (By way of comparison, National Express carries 16 million.) Shortly before it was acquired by First the company decided to focus on core routes and to invest in a major refurbishment programme to upgrade its 1,250-strong fleet and its terminals.

GREYHOUND
fits into the picture

Left: In the 1930s Greyhound seized on the art-deco style for its city terminals. This postcard shows an example in Toledo, Ohio, and features a 1932 Yellow Coach 670. It was posted in 1941, by which time the old-style 670 would have been replaced by the new generation of rear-engined coaches.

Above: Artwork for a 1935 advert featuring a normal-control Yellow Coach. Promoting fall and winter travel, it promised relaxation 'in a deeply cushioned chair, warm and secure, whatever the weather'.

This tells the tale of boarding a Greyhound bus in Norfolk, Virginia, then travelling through Carolina and Georgia where "we never was a minute late" — although the story takes a turn for the worse in Alabama when "that hound broke down and left us all stranded in downtown Birmingham".

But by then Greyhound's glory days had passed as car ownership rose, and the cost of air travel dropped.

Below: By 1937 coach design had changed dramatically, and this was reflected in Greyhound's advertising. In language which 70 years later seems distinctly quaint it calls on the woman illustrated to 'Get out of the frigid zone …' For an economy coming out of recession it also promotes cost saving: 'Greyhound travel costs only one-third as much as driving the average automobile'.

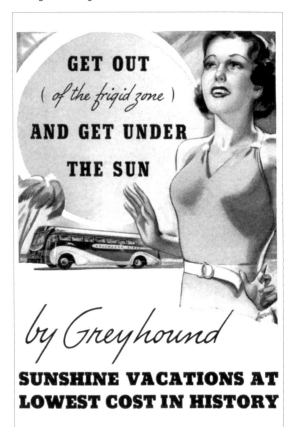

GET OUT
(of the frigid zone)
AND GET UNDER THE SUN

by Greyhound

SUNSHINE VACATIONS AT LOWEST COST IN HISTORY

Right and below right: There are large numbers of 1930s and 1940s postcards featuring Greyhound's art-deco terminals. Opened in 1937, this example in Louisville, Kentucky, was the first of many to be designed by the architect W. S. Arrasmith. Its facilities included dressing and bathrooms with a tub and shower. 1930s US postcards feature striking colour on otherwise realistic images, as a comparison between the postcard and a contemporary photograph shows.

Left: Southeastern Greyhound Lines produced this postcard in the late 1930s for passengers on two named De Luxe Florida Limited services — the Florida Sunshiner and the Florida Sun Chief — which it described as the 'finest, fastest and most luxurious bus service between Florida and the Mid-West'. The use of names for the services copied the practice of US railroads. The bus, an American Car & Foundries product, is superimposed on an image of Tennessee.

Right: The Union Bus Station in Jacksonville, Florida, is distinctly 1930s in design, as is the Greyhound Super-Coach parked outside. Union Bus Stations were terminals used by more than one operator — paralleling the existence of Union railroad stations in many cities.

Below: A 1938 advert suggesting that long-distance coach travel was attractive not just because it was cheap. The Yellow Coach illustrated marked a major advance in design, featuring integral construction and a rear-mounted engine, which could be petrol or diesel.

"If we were *Rolling in wealth*

we'd *still* travel GREYHOUND!

(even if it is the most economical way)"

"I SUPPOSE we'd go pretty high-hat if a rich uncle left us a million dollars ... costly cars, snappy clothes, fun and travel! But there are a few things that no amount of wealth would change, and one is our mode of travel.

"Pocket money will buy a Greyhound ticket to nearly anywhere on this continent—but a bankful of greenbacks couldn't duplicate what that ticket offers us.

"No sleek, special-built limousine can exceed the riding ease of a Greyhound Super-Coach with its brilliantly designed body, extra long wheelbase—its four-position reclining chairs, efficient ventilation and heating. No group of private chauffeurs can equal the National safety record set by Greyhound drivers.

"Mere money can't buy good fellowship, unusual human interest, and a fascinating close-up look at America, along its great highways. These come with each Greyhound trip, all included in the original low fare—a fraction the cost of driving a small private auto."

PRINCIPAL GREYHOUND INFORMATION OFFICES

Cleveland, O. , E. 9th & Superior
Philadelphia, Pennsylvania
    Broad St. Station
New York City . . 245 W. 50th St.
Chicago, Ill. . . . 12th & Wabash
Boston, Mass. . . 60 Park Square
Washington, D. C.
    1403 New York Ave. N.W.
Detroit, Michigan
    Washington Blvd. at Grand Riv.
St. Louis, Mo.
    Broadway & Delmar Boulevard
Charleston, W. Va.
    . . 155 Summers St.

San Francisco, Cal.
    Pine & Battery Sta.
Ft. Worth, Tex., 905 Commerce St.
Minneapolis, Minn.
    509 Sixth Avenue, N.
Memphis, Tenn. , 527 N. Main St.
New Orleans , La.
    400 N. Rampart St.
Lexington, Ky., 801 N. Limestone
Cincinnati, O. . . 630 Walnut St.
Richmond, Va., 412 E. Broad St.
Windsor, Ont., 405 Ouellette Ave.
London, Eng.. A. B. Reynoldson
    49 Leadenhall St.

The GREYHOUND LINES

Send for Popular Free Booklet "This Amazing America"
Here is one of the country's most popular travel booklets—with nearly 150 pictures and stories of strange and amazing places. Just mail this coupon to nearest information office listed at left. If you want bright pictorial folder and facts on trip to FLORIDA ☐, GULF COAST ☐, SOUTHWEST ☐, CALIFORNIA ☐, place check mark in proper space.

Name_____

Address_____

View of part of the San Francisco - Oakland Bay Bridge looking towards San Francisco. An outbound ocean going liner is just passing below the huge suspension span. In the foreground is one of Greyhound's New Super Coaches.

Come to San Francisco by GREYHOUND and see the world's Greatest Bridges

Left: The new Yellow Coach model let passengers sit high above 'vibration and road rumble'. This illustration was in a 1936 Pacific Greyhound timetable including such marathon cross-country runs as Los Angeles to New York, which left LA at 8.10am on Monday and arrived in NY at 9.55pm on Saturday.

Right: Baltimore, Maryland, was another Arrasmith-designed terminal, opened in 1942. It had 12 loading bays. Unrealistically elongated cars and a Yellow Coach 1930s Super Coach pass by on this postcard.

OVERLAND GREYHOUND BUS DEPOT. SIDNEY. NEBRASKA

Left: The next generation of rear-engined integrals wait outside the modest Overland Greyhound depot and air-conditioned café at Sidney, Nebraska. This style of coach was built in 1941/2, following which production was suspended until 1947. Roadside halts were common subjects for postcards in the 1930s and '40s.

Below: A promotional postcard for the new coach, captioned simply: 'I am Travelling on this Bus'. The publisher's code on the card points to it being a 1940 issue, at which time this was the future of coach travel.

Left: The Greyhound terminal in Charleston, West Virginia, was another fine art-deco confection, again with a Super-Coach in view. This card is postmarked September 1943, and the sender (presumably a Greyhound passenger) comments 'I nearly froze coming down', suggesting that coach heating wasn't all it might have been — hardly a ringing endorsement of coach travel.

IN ACTIVE SERVICE
for America's Two Great Armies!

There's a job to be done, and America's two great armies, military and civilian, are going to see it through. To speed that job, Greyhound Super-Coach travel now lends itself wholeheartedly to the needs of a nation at war.

Too young to serve in '17, the motor bus industry is now a powerful and willing defense force. With its immense carrying power and great flexibility, it is putting America's highways to work for America —smoothing out bottlenecks, rounding out the entire transportation picture. It is saving materials vital to national war effort by carrying far more people per gallon of fuel, per pound of rubber or metal, than do private automobiles.

What's more, motor buses are actively *in the war*, carrying thousands of selectees to military centers —other thousands of soldiers engaged in vital military movements.

To the men in the fighting forces—Greyhound's nation-wide service makes possible reunions with relatives, sweethearts and friends, whenever leaves and furloughs can be granted. It means precious moments saved by the most direct highway routes between military centers and homes.

To that other army—the rest of America's millions, all-out to back their fighting men—motor bus travel has become a vital necessity. It gets defense workers to jobs at decentralized projects— farmers to markets—teachers and students to school. It takes people of every occupation to their jobs and

homes in thousands of communities served by no other public transportation. It brings bright interludes of scenic enjoyment and recreation, so important in days of national stress . . . and all at travel cost within reach of every purse.

To both of these armies, Greyhound and the entire bus industry offer the extra edge of effort that America has every right to expect. Now every one of America's 55,000 motor buses has a new destination sign . . . *Victory for the U. S. A.!*

Mail Coupon to Nearest of these Greyhound Offices:
New York City • Cleveland, Ohio
Philadelphia, Penna • Chicago, Ill.
Fort Worth, Texas • Minneapolis,
Minn. • San Francisco, California
Boston, Mass. • Washington, D. C.

Detroit, Michigan • St. Louis, Mo.
Lexington, Kentucky • Charleston,
West Virginia • Cincinnati, Ohio
Richmond, Virginia • Memphis,
Tenn. • New Orleans, Louisiana

This brings full-color Defense Map of America
Just off the press, lithographed in full colors—fit for framing. Defense Map of America, showing hundreds of principal Army, Navy, Marine camps and bases . . . also information on military insignia, rank of officers and men. Just mail this coupon to nearest Greyhound Information Office, listed above.

LF-3

Name
Address

GREYHOUND

Above: In 1942 the Silversides featured in patriotic advertising which ended with the message: 'Now every one of America's 55,000 motor buses has a new destination sign ... Victory for the USA!' In the security-conscious 21st century it is interesting to note that a coupon on the page offers respondents a full-colour defence map of the USA 'showing hundreds of principal Army, Navy, Marine camps and bases' — not something, one imagines, of which today's Department of Homeland Security would approve.

Right: Billed as 'The bus that goes to sea', a GM Silversides crosses the seven-mile-long bridge between Miami and Key West. The caption on the reverse of the postcard describes the bridge as 'one of the world's scenic marvels and engineering achievements'. The original bridge had carried a railway and was rebuilt as a road bridge in the mid-1930s.

Right: During the war Greyhound developed a twin-deck design, seen here in a wartime advert which forecast: 'Super-coaches like this are coming, sure as Victory, to replace buses over-worked by the pressure of wartime travel.' Greyhound called this the GX-1, and one prototype was built in 1947. The driver sat high, on the upper deck. It is thought that the GX-1 never entered service.

Left: The Scenicruiser was the characteristic Greyhound coach of the 1950s. It was the first 40ft model and seated 43. The styling was by Raymond Loewy, a leading industrial designer who worked for Coca-Cola and car maker Studebaker, among other US household names. This is the 1949 GX-2 prototype, used to help promote the use of longer coaches. The caption on the reverse of this postcard describes the Scenicruiser as 'this beautiful new highway coach of exclusive Greyhound design'. Note the whitewall tyres.

Right: The production Scenicruiser, seen here in a 1950s postcard, appeared in 1954 and retained the general layout and appearance of the GX-2 but with a heavier look. Greyhound ordered 1,000, all of which were in service by 1956. The Scenicruiser had two engines — GM 4-71 units of 284cu in capacity — to give adequate power on hills. This proved troublesome, and from 1961 the coaches were rebuilt with single GM 8V-71 568cu in engines — a big and expensive job.

Turning back time

One of Britain's biggest bus collections is to be found at the Scottish Vintage Bus Museum in rural Fife. **Gavin Booth** charts its history.

It all started with a bus in a railway shed at North Berwick. The foundations of what has grown to be probably the largest bus museum in Britain, the Scottish Vintage Bus Museum at Lathalmond, were laid nearly 40 years ago in this unlikely setting.

Bus preservation in Scotland, as elsewhere in Britain, was a fairly lonely pursuit around 1970, regarded by many enthusiasts as something they certainly approved of but wouldn't know where to start when it came to restoring something as big as a bus. Where would we keep it and what would it all cost?

There had been bus-preservation pioneers in Scotland in the early 1960s. Bob Mackie had saved a 1932 Albion from the Alexander fleet, and a group of us were keen to save an ex-Hants & Dorset Leyland Titan TD1 that had survived with a contractor, but we really didn't know how to proceed, and the bus went for scrap. Out of that project grew the Albion Vehicle Preservation Trust, Scotland's pioneering preservation group, who rolled up their sleeves and got on with the job of preserving a 1950 Albion Valiant/Duple coach, learning as they went along.

Then Jasper Pettie arrived on the scene. Or rather arrived back on the scene. Scottish born and bred, Jasper had been working as an accountant in Canada and returned home to take up a post as Assistant Company Secretary at Scottish Omnibuses. We soon met as colleagues working within the Scottish Bus Group, but this was at a time when enthusiasts working for bus companies were wary of broadcasting their interest in case they were regarded as slightly weird. Which we maybe were.

Jasper took me to North Berwick to see his bus, a 1948 Guy Arab III with unusual Cravens bodywork that had finished its working life in the Alexander (Fife) fleet. Jasper had gained some experience of preservation during his Canadian sojourn and was keen to see permanent reminders of Scotland's transport heritage. It would become very clear as time moved on that he has a particular fondness for the once-giant Alexander empire and for Guy buses.

The buses that were coming off service around 1970 tended to be types bought in the 1950s — half-cab double-deckers and underfloor-engined single-deckers

Below left: The bus that started it all. Jasper Pettie's 1948 Guy Arab III with rare Cravens body stands outside the Alexander (Fife) central works in Kirkcaldy in 1975, having been repainted from Fife red into its original Alexander blue livery.

Right: Another early Leyland in the Jasper Pettie fleet is this 1934 Lion LT5A, rebodied by Alexander in 1946 and today restored in Perth 'town red' livery. In 1976 it took part in the London-Brighton run, being seen on Madeira Drive, Brighton.

— and there were some of us who regretted that we had missed out on the generation of buses we had grown up with, built in the 1930s and '40s, and even the iconic buses that we had heard and read of but had never really seen — the Leyland PLSC Lions and Leyland Titan TD1s, for instance. As bus preservation in Scotland grew, one unexpected outcome was that we would actually be able to see, ride on and occasionally even drive bus types that previously we had known only from photographs and fleet lists.

And much of this interest in pre-World War 2 buses has been sparked by Jasper. As he became more confident in his ability to restore older buses, often vehicles that appeared to be basket-cases on a one-way trip to Barnsley, he has built up the knowledge and expertise to transform heaps of rotting wood and metal into active, pristine vehicles. But he would be the first to point out that this was not by any means a one-man exercise. The preservation movement in Scotland is well served by people who can turn their hand to literally every aspect of bus preservation.

All of which is a long preamble to the story of the Scottish Vintage Bus Museum. But enterprises like Lathalmond don't just happen overnight, and Jasper's vision and energy are an important part of the story.

From North Berwick Jasper bought premises at Pathhead, south of Edinburgh. This provided minimal covered accommodation and a sizeable yard, and as Jasper's collection of buses grew, so did a team of volunteers who wanted to get into bus preservation but lacked the resources and experience. What was becoming known as JPC, the Jasper Pettie

Consortium, gave these keen enthusiasts experience of bus engines, gearboxes, axles, electrics, bodywork, paintwork — and it could be a bit hit and miss, because most were unskilled and were learning as they went along. The fact that many now own and restore their own vintage buses is a direct result of the many evenings and weekends they spent at Pathhead.

The JPC quickly outgrew the Pathhead premises and bought a new, larger site at Whitburn, in West Lothian. Here were sizeable premises with much more covered accommodation, and this allowed the collection to increase. The growing interest in bus preservation, helped by the annual Open Days that were staged at Whitburn, attracted more volunteers as well as vehicle owners seeking that most elusive resource — covered accommodation for their buses.

The Whitburn site had previously been used by a road haulier and was attractive because of its proximity to the M8 motorway and the rest of the Scottish road network. This prompted a dairy company to approach what had now become the Scottish Vintage Bus Museum to explore the possibility of buying the site as a distribution depot. The idea was attractive, not least because of the money that was on the table, but SVBM had to find a new site, and quickly.

After much searching a potential site was identified in Fife. This was the former Royal Navy stores depot at Lathalmond, situated in open countryside north of Dunfermline. In its heyday Lathalmond had supplied the nearby naval base and dockyard at Rosyth, on the Firth of Forth. The 1994 closure of the base rendered the site superfluous for naval use, and it was put on

Above: A selection of buses lined up in the yard of the Pathhead premises in March 1978. Some survived and can be seen at Lathalmond, but others were broken up to provide spare parts for other projects.

Below: The 1929 Leyland Tiger TS2/Alexander, P63 in the Alexander fleet, emerges from the Pathhead shed in February 1981 under its own power for the first time following restoration.

Right: This 1942 unfrozen Leyland Titan TD5 with Leyland-style Alexander body was another early Pettie restoration project. Converted by Scottish Omnibuses for use as an open-topper, it gained a new roof based on one that had previously been fitted to a Ribble Leyland PD2 and was repainted into SMT's pre-1949 blue livery.

Left: Jasper Pettie's fondness for Guy Arabs manifested itself in the purchase of this 1950 Arab III with Guy body, seen at the Dunbar Rally in 1980 painted in Western SMT livery but nowadays correctly presented as a Central SMT bus.

Left: Double-deck line-up at the 1988 Whitburn open day, comprising, from left, an Edinburgh Guy Arab/Duple, an Alexander Guy Arab III/Cravens, an SMT Leyland Titan TD5, an Alexander Leyland Titan PD2, a Scottish Omnibuses Bristol Lodekka and a Glasgow Leyland PD2.

the market. The site offered a network of tarmac roads, together with sheds that had been used for storage, and other buildings used for administration. With money in its pocket SVBM bid unsuccessfully for the whole 90-acre site but then bought around half of it back from its new owners.

I can still vividly recall standing at Lathalmond on a cold Boxing Day 1994 looking at this bleak and lifeless site and trying, with the others gathered there, to imagine that this could become a viable bus museum. The potential was clearly there — covered accommodation for every bus that could want it (we thought) and a private road system to test the buses and offer rides to the public — but it seemed like a massive job to transform it.

It was, of course. Moving the 60-odd buses housed at Whitburn across to Fife was a major logistical exercise, yet with proper planning and not a little ingenuity it was done in time for an inaugural Open Weekend to be held at Lathalmond in September 1995. Remember that by no means all of the buses making the journey were runners, and some were in a very delicate 'as found' condition.

A workshop shed was quickly identified, and, in addition to large sheds for deep storage of buses that would be in line for restoration at some later stage, there had to be sheds for the runners — the buses that appeared at rallies and other events and were increasingly in demand for film and television work. A requirement for a display hall to exhibit the restored vehicles was soon satisfied, and over the years discrete areas for bodybuilding and painting have been created. The demand for space in the workshops is such that buses must be under active restoration if they are to justify the use of the space.

And this is the ideal place to say a bit about the workshops. Many bus operators would be happy to have workshops like Lathalmond's — and many Traffic Commissioners would be happy if they did. SVBM recognised the importance of a properly planned, properly equipped and properly run workshop area, and that is what it has created. The 14 working bays in the 20,000sq ft building give vehicle owners a bright working environment, along with access to a full-ring air system and a range of air tools, Hywema lifting posts, wood and sheet-metal benches, guillotines, welding equipment, engine cranes and body lifts. The main parts store is in a separate building nearby, but fast-moving parts are kept in the workshop.

Much of the equipment has come from major bus companies in Scotland when they have been updating their own workshops, and Lathalmond has an enviable store of chassis, engine and body parts, often items donated by bus companies when clearing out what to them were obsolete parts.

The success of the workshop can be measured by the 1999 decision to create a second workshop in an adjacent building, and this is used for bodywork and minor repairs, while the main workshop continues to handle major work.

While some bus museums follow a policy of concentrating their resources on one major restoration before moving on to another, the majority of the buses and coaches at Lathalmond are owned by individuals or groups rather than the SVBM, and so there are many projects making progress at different speeds. This can mean that the museum can't always provide a 'new' vehicle to order for its regular May and August open events, but there are always tantalising glimpses of work in progress that provide something to look forward to.

And that work is not just on buses, as Lathalmond provides a home for the Shed 47 Railway Restoration Group, which created a workshop in the former locomotive shed that was used when the naval stores were connected to the railway network. Here volunteers undertake restoration work on railway locomotives and rolling stock, and there is a short length of test track.

But buses are what Lathalmond is mainly about, and mainly but not exclusively Scottish buses. The great majority have a Scottish connection, having either been originally owned and operated by Scottish companies or having a more unusual connection, like the 1947 Albion Venturer (Scottish-built) that returned from Australia for restoration.

The museum formalised its aims some years ago when it gained registered-charity status and is run by a management committee consisting of the trustees and committed members. SVBM is run on a purely voluntary basis, and individuals and groups will regularly be found working on their vehicles. Several of the young men who got their hands dirty at Pathhead all those years ago are still actively involved at Lathalmond, and Jasper Pettie is keen to acknowledge the part they have played in the whole saga. David Heathcote, another pioneering Scottish bus preservationist, has chaired SVBM since its inception, and other long-serving stalwarts include Graeme Fraser, Eddie Taylor and a growing band of younger preservationists whose first-hand memories of buses date back only to what the old-stagers might regard as modern buses — rear-engined double-deckers and Leyland Nationals, for example.

An important and often costly aspect of owning premises like Lathalmond is the constant need to maintain and improve the buildings, roadways and grounds to ensure that everything is safe, secure and weatherproof. Regular income is provided by vehicle owners who rent space for their vehicles and is boosted by the May and August open days and the use of the premises by other organisations, attracted by the space and facilities on offer. There is a shop selling a wide range of transport-related items, as well as a café in the display hall.

Although Lathalmond houses buses and coaches that date back little more than 20 years, it is the significant proportion of older buses that many regard as the star exhibits. There are some 20 prewar and wartime buses, as well as tow wagons and chassis from this era, and although buses from this period are inevitably at least 60 years old, they are still turning up. Some years ago a 1935 SMT Cowieson body was discovered in Wales, recovered and brought to Lathalmond where the body is being reconstructed, mounted on a Leyland Tiger TS7 chassis. More recently a 1936 Western SMT Leyland Cheetah with full-front Alexander body was found in Shropshire, and this too was rescued and brought back north. The Cheetah could well be a long-term project, but, like other vehicles at Lathalmond, it is safely under cover for future attention.

The Cheetah rescue was led by Jasper Pettie, whose original fleet of one (the Cravens-bodied Guy Arab III) had in the meantime grown to 12 — all Guy Arabs and prewar Leylands. Jasper is quick to acknowledge the help of others in restoring his fleet,

including Roland Williams and Tam Loggie, both former bus-industry professionals who are based at Lathalmond and undertake work for a range of vehicle owners.

A full list of buses normally housed at Lathalmond is on the museum website (www.busweb.co.uk/svbm), but it is worth identifying a few of the star attractions; these are my favourites, I should add, and readers will have their own preferences.

Two buses that certainly fall into the 'I never thought I'd see one of them' category are Alexander P63, the 1929 Leyland Tiger TS2/Alexander, and Glasgow Corporation 111, the 1928 all-Leyland Titan TD1. I am looking forward to seeing SMT H110, the 1935 Leyland Tiger TS7 with the rescued Cowieson body, which is making good progress in the workshops, and I never fail to enjoy the sight and sounds of CDR 679, the Guy Arab II/Duple now painted in AA Motor Services green and cream.

My fondness for Edinburgh buses is satisfied by a growing fleet of these, ranging from the ex-London Transport Guy Arab rebodied by Duple Nudd, right through to Lothian Leyland Olympians. Nearing completion after a long restoration is Edinburgh

Below: The fine Glasgow Corporation all-Leyland Titan TD1, No 111, back in its home city for its 1994 launch.

Left: One of the 60 utility Guy Arabs originally delivered to London Transport that were bought by Edinburgh Corporation and rebodied by Duple Nudd in 1952/3 was saved and rebuilt to its 1953 form. It is seen at Silverknowes, with the Firth of Forth in the background, taking part in an Edinburgh Classic Bus Running Day.

Bottom left: Now residing close to its original operating territory, a former Alexander (Fife) 1964 Bristol Lodekka FS6G/ECW, seen at Lathalmond in 2001.

Below: The Albion Venturer CX19 with Comeng body that was built for DRTT, Sydney, in 1947 is seen at the 2006 Lathalmond Open Weekend following its restoration.

Corporation 798, one of the infamous MCW Orion-bodied Leyland Titan PD2/20s, which is getting the same thorough treatment from the Scoular father-and-son team as the famous three-door Leyland Leopard/Alexander, 101. The Scoulars' next project is moving on, a 1929 Leyland Lion PLSC3 new to Hants & Dorset.

As the years have passed the Lathalmond collection has been joined by buses from the 1960s and '70s, like ex-Scottish Bus Group Leyland Leopards, Seddon Pennines, Daimler Fleetlines and Volvo Ailsas, and in addition to the Sydney Albion there is an Alexander-bodied Guy Victory which returned to Scotland after service in Hong Kong.

Things don't stand still at Lathalmond, and the management committee is constantly looking at ways to improve the facilities. A function room has been

created to cater for the museum's social side, and although it seemed unlikely on that cold Boxing Day in 1994, the existing sheds are filled to capacity, and consideration is being given to expanding the storage space and creating new visitor attractions.

In addition to full-size vehicles SVBM is amassing a range of bus-associated items like uniforms, badges, ticket machines, timetables, notices, photographs and books, and Lathalmond would seem to be a natural place for an archive of the Scottish bus industry.

The museum is less than an hour's drive from Edinburgh, heading north across the Forth Road Bridge to Junction 4 of the M90, then west on the B914 and B915 roads. The main public days are the May Running Day and the August Open Weekend, when bus services using vintage vehicles are available between Dunfermline and the museum, and within the

This line-up in 2003 gives an idea of the range of vehicles that can be seen at Lathalmond. From the left are a 1945 Aberdeen Corporation Daimler CWD6/Duple, a 1960 A1 Service Daimler CVG6LX-30/Northern Counties, a 1981 Alexander (Midland) Leyland National 2, a 1971 Eastern Scottish Daimler Fleetline CRG6/ECW and a 1950 McGill's Guy Arab III/Duple.

museum premises. On Sundays from Easter to the end of September the museum's Guide Sunday facility provides visitors with guided tours of the museum premises.

SVBM is in the enviable position of having extensive premises, good covered accommodation and scope to expand. Although the initial impetus came from Jasper Pettie, his fellow trustees and the management committee have dealt with the museum in a sensible and business-like way, so that under their stewardship it continues to improve and surprise. Lathalmond — and, for those enthusiasts who seem to have difficulty with the site's name, it's pronounced 'LathAHmond' — is a treasure-house for people like myself and the editor of this *Yearbook*. And even if you can't claim any Scottish roots, it's worth a visit just to marvel at what can be done and what has been done.

Riding on a Regent

Remember the days of AEC Regents? **David Wayman** takes a trip back in time, to the late 1950s in North East England.

In our imagination we're going on a complex sequence of journeys. You'll enjoy it. Plenty of nice scenery: smoky chimneys, pit-head gear and slag heaps, not to mention noise from grimy shipyards and engineering works.

Our double-deck bus, now eight years old and member of an octet, is a gorgeous navy-blue and white 1950 AEC Regent Mark III, type 9612A, with superb 56-seat Roe teak-framed body featuring that manufacturer's 'safety' staircase incorporating two landings. It's from the 109-strong fleet of the Sunderland District Omnibus Company (SDO), based in the mining village of Philadelphia, which is in the Urban District of Houghton-le-Spring (population 31,000) in County Durham.

Yes, most of the villages hereabouts are 'mining', and long may they be so. We'll just love riding on the Regent because it has good performance and will emit some delightful, euphonious sounds from its 9.6-litre engine and four-speed crash gearbox. A lot of bus fans say these are their favourites now that there are no 1940 Leyland Titan TD7s in the fleet.

The 4½-hour outing involves integrated services 49 and 95, operated jointly by SDO and the Gateshead-based 680-vehicle Northern General Transport Company, which is in the British Electric Traction group and since 1931 has owned all SDO shares. The interworked sequence of journeys goes like this:

- 49: Easington Lane–Herrington Burn–Sunderland–Newcastle, returning as
- 95: Newcastle–Sunderland–Herrington Burn–Fencehouses, returning as
- 95: Fencehouses–Herrington Burn–Sunderland, returning as
- 49: Sunderland–Herrington Burn–Easington Lane.

Below: Here's one of our AEC Regents when new, in Park Lane, Sunderland, in the days before the bus station and with an as-yet incomplete advertisement for Littlewood's pools. But who put the dent in the upper-saloon side panel? Oh, heinous crime! He'd have had to answer to the General Manager, Mr E. S. Mountain, and would never have got over it. *David Wayman collection*

Right: Seen here at Houghton-le-Spring is a 7-litre Gardner 5LW-powered Guy Arab IV with lightweight 63-seat Metro-Cammell Orion bodywork with platform doors, typifying Northern's contribution to the longer-distance jointly operated services during the late 1950s. *R. F. Mack*

The journey sequence isn't followed on Saturdays, when services 49/95 don't go north of Sunderland, and no journeys on the 49 go south of Houghton town centre to Easington Lane after 11.21am. On Sundays the sequence starts later but is otherwise the same as on weekdays.

The Sunday–Friday vehicle requirement is for nine double-deckers — six from SDO and three from Northern's Sunderland depot. Northern always uses 7 litre Gardner 5LW-powered Guy Arabs, of which it has 201 (plus 18 Leyland Titans) in its double-deck fleet.

So here we are on a weekday at Easington Lane. It's noon, and our Regent, visiting for the second time today on its duty, is working the 12.10 to Newcastle on the half-hourly service 49. Mind you, nobody travels to Newcastle from Easington Lane on the 49, because it takes 92 minutes for the 22.6 miles via Sunderland, although Newcastle is only 14 miles away as the crow flies.

Folk can get there in 62 minutes on a number 45 bus (West Hartlepool to Newcastle via Chester-le-Street) or 65 minutes on a 39 (Murton or Thornley to Newcastle via Washington). Service 45 is operated jointly by Northern and the Darlington-based United Automobile Services, usually with Guy and Tilling-red Bristol double-deckers respectively. United is a British Transport Commission undertaking with a fleet of some 1,060 vehicles. Northern and SDO operate service 39 jointly, normally using Leyland Royal Tigers or Tiger Cubs.

In order to avoid confusion with services 39 and 45, Newcastle-bound buses on service 49 show 'Sunderland' on their blinds until reaching East Herrington, where the setting is changed to 'Newcastle'. However, while other services approaching Sunderland town centre from the south-west stay on the A690 Durham Road, services 49/95 turn right from that highway to use the marginally longer route via Alexandra Road and Tunstall Road. SDO buses with bodies built before 1951 don't have a service number blind and so when going to Sunderland by this route their destination blinds simply show 'via Tunstall Rd', as there isn't room to squeeze in 'Sunderland' as well.

Aboard our Regent we'll take the A182 road, going the same way as the 45 to where it turns left at Houghton centre. We'll remain on the A182 with service 39 through Newbottle to Herrington Burn. The blue saloons of the independent Trimdon Motor Services also use the A182 on part of their Trimdon Village–Houghton route.

Away we go north from Easington Lane with a convulsing start. Lovely! We're leaving behind the United saloon that'll set off at 12.15 on service 18 (Easington Lane to Spennymoor). We amble along, stopping and starting … and now here we are at Hetton-le-Hole (1.1 miles). We keep straight on to the centre of Houghton (2.3 miles, due at 12.22), where the A182 road forms a scissors junction with the A690 linking Durham with Sunderland. Houghton, which we pronounce as the Old English 'hoh tun' ('hill-spur farm'), is an interchange point for no fewer than 11 services.

Now we have another deliciously juddering take-off. We continue north and shortly ascend Newbottle Bank. Blending with delightful orchestration from the Regent's cog-box, the 9.6-litre engine takes it in its stride without the raucous effect of SDO's Strachans-bodied 7.7-litre AEC Regals, all eight of which were withdrawn last year when only nine years old.

Above: This 44-seat Saro-bodied 5.76-litre Leyland Tiger Cub in the Northern fleet is seen when new in 1954 at Houghton *en route* to Newcastle via Washington on service 39. Low bridges at Penshaw station precluded the use of double-deckers. *David Wayman collection*

SDO's Regents, along with six contemporary 9.8-litre Leyland Titan PD2/1s with similar bodywork, exude an air of superiority over Northern's Guys. Of course those Arabs are extremely reliable and economical, but ever so slow on some of the banks where Regents and PD2s just romp! A handful of SDO buses are 5LW Guy Arabs, incidentally.

Now paralleling service 50 as well as 14, we reach Newbottle (due at 12.28), where buses on service 95 come up from Fencehouses, nine minutes to the west. Those on the 14 turn eastward to reach the A690 at Stoneygate.

On the common 49/95 section between Newbottle and Sunderland via Herrington Burn the basic frequency is a severely lopsided one, differing according to direction. Buses to Sunderland run at intervals of 12 and 18 minutes, and those from Sunderland at nine- and 21-minute intervals. That means two every half hour each way. From Newbottle we keep going north like the 39 and 50 and at the beginning of a fairly long descent look ahead to Philadelphia, site of SDO's depot. Some local people still call it 'Fillydelfer'.

The company had its own power station for the trams it operated until 1925. I bet it wishes it could produce its own diesel fuel now. The advent of electricity must have made a big impression locally, because on our way down we pass Electric Crescent and Voltage Terrace. And what we see rising from the multitude of domestic chimneys is almost certainly smoke from miners' concessionary coal.

Just past the bus depot the Houghton–Barnwell service (52) joins us from Junction Row, and at 12.32 we come to Herrington Burn (4.2 miles), another bus junction. The 39 and 52 go ahead, but we, like the 50 and 95, turn sharp right to head east on the fairly straight and flat B1286 road to East Herrington (5.9 miles, due at 12.39), in Sunderland Rural District.

This is where we meet the A690 road again, turning left onto it. We climb gently to the boundary of the County Borough of Sunderland (population 182,000) and can see the sea some four miles away. There now follows a hurried north-easterly descent of the Durham Road dual carriageway, where between 1949 and 1954 Corporation trams ran in the central reservation.

As we progress through the town we'll note Northern buses on some services operated jointly with Sunderland Corporation, which undertaking's 176 green-and-cream buses are mostly Daimlers and Guys. We won't look at them in detail.

Now we zoom through the Plains Farm dip and then rise up before plunging down the 700yd, 1-in-14 Humbledon Bank. This is where we leave Durham Road and turn right into Alexandra Road, then cross the path of SDO's service 51 and pass Bainbridge Avenue at 12.49. Now penetrating the sedate and genteel inner suburbs of Ashbrooke and Thornhill, we're joined by SDO local service 38 as we turn left into Tunstall Road.

SDO began operating through this district in unusual circumstances. During 1925, when part of the main road to Durham was closed for a tramway extension to the foot of Humbledon Bank, SDO buses were diverted along Alexandra Road and Tunstall Road, where they stopped to pick up local passengers. Of below-average population density, this neighbourhood was hardly viable tramway territory, but after the reopening of Durham Road SDO continued to route some buses this way. Then, following an approach in 1926 by Sunderland Corporation, which at that time was not

Right: Crews called them 'loaf tins'. They were 30ft long and 8ft wide and were assembled by Northern in the period 1952-4 using prewar AEC 7.7-litre engines and other running units, and fitted with austere 43-seat bodywork by Picktree of Chester-le-Street. Rough, raucous, noisy and harsh they certainly were. Wonderful! This one stands in the newly opened Park Lane bus station in Sunderland before setting off for Hebburn via Jarrow.
David Wayman collection

Left: Here's a scene from the early 1950s, when service 49 was exclusively SDO-operated, before being integrated with service 95 and shared with Northern. In Union Street, alongside Sunderland's bomb-scarred railway station, a new 43-seat Brush-bodied 9.8-litre Royal Tiger loads behind a 32-seat Roe-bodied 8.6-litre Tiger TS8 of 1938. The latter is probably on a short-working, and its blind has not been reset.
S. E. Letts

Right: It's a long way to Bishop Auckland, especially from Sunderland on service 57 aboard a five-cylinder utility Guy — 24 miles, in fact. Yes, it would get there all right, going down banks like the 1 in 8 of Houghton Cut and those of 1 in 9 and 1 in 12 at Durham. But then, of course, it had to come back up! The bus is a 1945 Northern Counties-bodied Arab II in the SDO fleet, fitted postwar (we hope) with upholstered seats in place of its wooden-slatted originals. *Roy Marshall*

empowered to operate motor buses, SDO commenced the local service that later became the 38.

So we come tearing into Park Lane bus station (10.7 miles), opened the year before last, and from where we're due out at 12.58. We see loads of Northern Guy Arabs, mostly 'deckers, and some AEC saloons, plus Bristols of United and Durham District. There are other SDO vehicles, of course, not only Regent IIIs and Titan PD2s but older PD1s, along with more of the lovely single-deck Royal Tigers plus some Tiger Cubs, and maybe we'll spot a few earlier Tigers of types PS1 and PS2.

There are still a couple of SDO wartime Guys with original bodies pottering about, plus a similar one that's unusual because SDO has hired it from Northern and it's in Gateshead & District maroon but with a Northern fleet number. There are also four hired Northern postwar Guys in SDO colours, plus SDO's own four rebodied wartime ones. It's rumoured that SDO will shortly be getting some new, longer Leyland 'deckers, which will replace all the hired stuff along with the unrebodied utilities and a few PD1s.

Our driver and conductor have dashed into the Northern canteen, in which by tradition their intake of strong tea will be slurped hurriedly from the saucer.

Below: With Binns' new store being built behind on the site of the one that was bombed, the delectable object in the foreground in Waterloo Place, Sunderland, is a 56-seat all-Leyland Titan PD2/3 of 1951. It is one of four from the Gateshead & District fleet, hired to Northern during 1952 but retaining its G&D fleet number for three months before acquisition by Northern. *David Wayman collection*

The Regent picks up a fair load and soon we set off northbound. From here the Sunderland–Newcastle section of services 49/95 is integrated with the same section of service 40 on a 15-minute frequency throughout the day Monday to Friday and from 12.29pm on Sunday.

During most of Saturday there's a 10-minute frequency with service 40 only. The 40 is operated by United, Northern and SDO, and the full route is Middlesbrough– Newcastle, although there are no journeys right through, as the service is generally run in two overlapping parts. These are Middlesbrough– West Hartlepool–Sunderland and West Hartlepool–Sunderland–Newcastle, with short workings. On the 40, only United operates south of West Hartlepool, and only Northern and SDO operate north of Sunderland.

Northern usually runs a couple of Park Royal-bodied Leyland Titan PD2s among the Guy Arabs on West Hartlepool–Newcastle journeys on service 40. The Leylands and some of the Guys have platform doors. SDO normally also runs lightweight 1955 Metro-Cammell Orion-bodied Leyland Titan PD2/12s. They weigh only 6 tons 17cwt 2qr unladen, and, by heavens, do they not bounce like a rubber ball when empty! Aye, and they tremble like jelly when idling too, but, man, you should see them go!

Just after leaving the bus station we pass the Northern depot and then the terminus of the Economic Bus Service run by G. R. Anderson and E. W. Wilson of Whitburn, each with his own fleet of maroon-and-cream saloons, mostly AECs and Leylands. They run two busy coast-road services to South Shields. Within a further half minute we're passing the end of Waterloo

Place, where journeys in both directions on service 95 either call or terminate, and southbound 49 journeys begin.

Now we're leaving the town centre by the A19 road and heading north across the River Wear on Wearmouth Bridge. This takes us from the parish of Bishopwearmouth into Monkwearmouth, where in 667AD there was born a lad who joined the nearby monastery and later, at Jarrow, was to write *The Ecclesiastical History of the English People* and other stuff. That's right, his name was Bede, but, no, that wasn't him hopping on a number 26 bus in Park Lane. Incidentally, in his day the township on the south side of the Wear was regarded as the 'sundered' land, separated by the water, hence the name 'Sunderland', which eventually covered a much wider area. Ocean-going ships can pass under the bridge, and on the seaward and landward sides of it along the river there are shipyards, engineering works, docks, quays and coal staiths.

Now here's the Wheat Sheaf junction and next, we're in Newcastle Road … and now we're at Fulwell Mill. From here, on favourable gradients, we whizz past Herbert Terrace, where the 'Shields-bound buses on service 14 bear right, and stay on the A19. We bear left to head north-westerly on the A184 into Boldon Urban District, past the sanatorium and the dog track, reaching East Boldon at 1.13 (14.8 miles). After the main stop at Black's Corner, where we're joined by service 90 to Newcastle, we climb gently to enter West

Boldon, being due there 1.17. We negotiate the gentle reverse curves of Addison Road before plummeting down the short, steep bank.

Rounding the right-hand bend we come to the level crossing, and if we're lucky we'll see a BR Standard Class 9F 2-10-0 thrashing its way from Tyne Dock to Consett with a load of iron ore. The gates are open for us, so our Regent will continue its gallop along the flat and fairly straight stretch ahead. Aye, there's Scott's House on the left and next, Follonsby Terrace … and now we're coming to White Mare Pool (18.3 miles). Oh, what an awkward junction! It's something like a letter 'Y', on which we go up the stem and turn on to the left prong, which is a narrow railway bridge; the right-hand prong is the A185 road from South Shields. See, there's three-way traffic-light control. And you seem to wait ages if you catch them just changing to red.

Now we're entering Wardley, which is in Felling Urban District, in which 25,000 folk live. Here, working a joint service, we'll see the yellow-and-cream vehicles of Newcastle Corporation and the dark-maroon-and-

Above: It might have a Brush body but it won't go sweeping up to its terminus, for it has to climb Gateshead High Street and then part of the notorious Wrekenton Bank. With 5LW power and an unladen weight of exactly 8 tons, a Gateshead & District 56-seat 1950 Guy Arab III in the sombre livery of dark maroon with little relief ambles through Newcastle on a cross-Tyne service. *R. F. Mack*

cream ones of SDO's related company, Gateshead & District, which may look like a municipal system but isn't. Newcastle has 250 motor buses, mostly AECs and Leylands, and, confined to the north of the Tyne, 186 BUT and Sunbeam trolleybuses. G&D's fleet of 70 comprises 37 7-litre 5LW Guy Arabs and 33 9.8-litre Leyland Titan PD2s. Spot the difference! We attack the sharp bank — and just listen to that symphony from the engine and 'box down below as our pilot drops it to third! Yes, the Regent will make it, but the five-cylinder Guys with which our Regent consorts usually need a further down-change, to second.

Now, although we greatly enjoy riding on crash-'box Regent IIIs, as the woman next door says, 'I never indulge in gossip but just listen to this!' Rumour has it that the SDO fleet engineer's not quite so enamoured of them. No, because it seems that the gearbox is of a 1929 design. It was never meant for the torque of an engine as big as the 9.6-litre diesel, and all too often these Regents are out of service for the replacement of second-speed layshafts — which the company sometimes has to wait for!

What's more, someone has calculated that a Gardner 5LW can give up to 10% better fuel consumption than an AEC 9.6 or a Leyland 9.8 in a bus of similar weight, along with maintenance costs that are lower by at least the same percentage. Here's another thing: they reckon there's concern about the rate that those delectable SDO Royal Tigers go through front tyres and brake linings too, as well as fuel! I dunno; just telling you what I've heard.

Next we rush down to Heworth, (due there at 1.29),

where we don't see ancient trams at the terminus on the right any more. We press on, along Ridley Terrace and past Felling railway station, among much grime-caked industrial scenery. But glimpses across to the north bank of the Tyne, to the right, reveal hundreds of terraced house roofs that glisten like jewels when they're wet.

We enter the County Borough of Gateshead, from Bede's Latin description translated into English as 'at the place of the goat's head', now home to 115,000 souls. Soon we observe G&D's Sunderland Road depot on our right. The town has some long, steep hills for those doughty 5LWs! Now (21.5 miles) here's the junction where we join the A1 — aye, the Great North Road — where yet more services merge with ours.

At the foot of High Street we start the jaunt across the Tyne Bridge. This takes us into the Northumbrian city of Newcastle upon Tyne (no hyphens, please!), populated by 291,000 Novocastrians and others, and site of a new castle built in the 11th century. We turn right and go down City Road, then left and under Manors station to reach Worswick Street bus station (21.6 miles, pronounced Wurzick), with its cramped and awkward diagonal platforms rising steeply to the road, where we're due in at 1.42.

It wouldn't be the first bus to run back into the wall, so the driver will put the handbrake fully on and leave first gear engaged while the conductor puts the chock under the nearside front wheel. Both men will then disappear for a minute or two. Sorry, there's no time to hop off and see Newcastle's other main attractions, the bus stations at Marlborough Crescent, Haymarket, Croft Street, Carliol Street and Manors Bus Park, at least not if we are to stay with the Regent. It has only two minutes' scheduled layover time here, and then it's out again for Fencehouses (Lambton 'D' Pit) at 1.44 on service 95.

After that it'll work the 3.07 journey back from Fencehouses (service 95) and then the 3.48 from Sunderland (service 49), arriving in Easington Lane at 4.35 before starting all over again at 4.40. By that time we'll be dehydrated as well as saddle-sore. The Regent, however, will pay two further visits to Worswick Street today, the last one for the 10.44 Newcastle–Herrington Burn (near Philadelphia depot) on service 95, its final journey.

Talk about maximising vehicle use! That's the way to do it.

Right: Here we are at Newcastle's awkward and cramped Worswick Street bus station, and the chock is firmly under that nearside front wheel. On service 40 but using the same stand as our bus and sharing its route over the 12 miles from Sunderland, Northern's new 5LW Guy Arab III with Newcastle-built 56-seat Northern Coachbuilders body has pulled well up the stand, as they did, and loads in the evening sunshine in 1950. *A. B. Cross*

Tight scheduling by SDO — the day's bus workings for an AEC Regent on the 49/95 services. The bus is idle for a total of just 43 minutes in a working day of 16 hours 49 minutes.

Service No	49	95	49	95	49	95	49	95
Newcastle	–	9.14	–	1.44	–	6.14	–	10.44
Sunderland	–	9.57	11.18	2.27	3.48	6.57	8.18	11.27
Herrington Burn	7.13	10.22	11.43	2.52	4.13	7.22	8.43	11.52
Fencehouses	–	10.35	–	3.05	–	7.35	–	–
Easington Lane	7.35	–	12.05	–	4.35	–	9.05	–
Easington Lane	7.40	–	12.10	–	4.40	–	9.10	
Fencehouses	–	10.37	–	3.07	—	7.37	–	
Herrington Burn	8.02	10.50	12.32	3.20	5.02	7.50	9.32	
Sunderland	8.28	11.15	12.58	3.45	5.28	8.15	9.58	
Newcastle	9.12	–	1.42	–	6.12	–	10.42	

Hong Kong, 10 years on

Ten years after the end of British rule **Peter Rowlands** went to Hong Kong. Here he offers a visitor's-eye view of the bus scene there.

All photographs by the author

Nothing can prepare you for this — not even a lifetime of expectation. Picture the biggest double-decker buses you can imagine, three axles each and three abreast, charging down a broad city-centre boulevard at 40 miles an hour: not just the three at the front, but three more behind them, and three more after that … and then still more, in seemingly endless procession. The effect is breathtaking.

This is Hong Kong, and, whatever you thought it would be like, it's more. The buses are longer, smarter, cleaner, fuller … more everything than you ever thought they would be. The buildings are taller. The streets are simply more Chinese.

And yet, not entirely. Everything about the environment speaks West — the brashness of the signing, the international brands and the brisk, businesslike bustle. Hong Kong may have been technically reunited with China for 10 years now, but, visually speaking, little has changed in that time. It's still an extraordinary place, where Westerners and Chinese can feel equally comfortable.

What is not so familiar is the sparkling cleanliness of the buses — especially those of the Kowloon Motor Bus fleet. No graffiti, no etched windows, no vandalised seats — not in my limited experience, anyway, though locals might tell you otherwise. To a visitor from London every vehicle looks as if it came through a wash this morning and out of the paint shop last week. This, you feel, is a city of politeness, of respect; one where a high value is attached to public transport. It reminds you of some of the things that the West seems to have lost.

Only one bus operator remains of the two that we grew up reading about. Kowloon Motor Bus (KMB), the survivor, is in fact now one of the biggest double-deck-bus operators in the world, with a fleet of over 4,000 vehicles — mostly three-axle double-deckers. Yes, *four thousand*.

The other operator of the past, China Motor Bus, disappeared during the 1990s: not with a bang, but gradually, in what is now seen by some as almost a loss of heart. Following its demise there was much jostling before the new order emerged. What you see

now is effectively a restored duopoly of franchised operators, featuring KMB and NWS.

NWS controls two main subsidiaries — Citybus, with its yellow, red and blue livery, and New World First Bus, in white, orange and green. UK-based FirstGroup had a hand in setting up New World First Bus in 1998 but sold out its quarter share in 2000. Similarly Stagecoach briefly owned Citybus, but then it also withdrew.

Hong Kong is divided into three main areas. The island itself lies just south of Kowloon, a spit of land connected to the Chinese mainland. These two locations are linked by a 10-minute ride on the famous Star Ferry and share what you might call Hong Kong's downtown area. For a visitor it's hard to pinpoint the differences between the two environments, but the island has the financial district, with the lion's share of sparkling skyscrapers, while Kowloon has more of the elegant shops. To the north of Kowloon lie the much larger but more-thinly populated New Territories.

Simplistically, Citybus and New World operate on the island, while KMB operates in Kowloon and the New Territories. In practice, however, all three operators' vehicles intermingle on both sides of the water. The progressive building and improvement of road tunnels between the island and the mainland have made cross-working easier to arrange, though I read that actual route-sharing between operators is no longer favoured here.

It's when you get a feel for the sheer teeming population of urban Hong Kong, still crammed into an area far smaller than you'd think could possibly work, that you start to understand why they need three-axle double-decker buses. There simply wouldn't be room for everyone to drive private cars. Although there's now a sparkling metro system, buses are still the main means of getting about, and they can seem full at any time of day.

The paradox is that although the place is so crowded, traffic congestion seems no worse than elsewhere, and the streets are surprisingly wide — especially in Kowloon, which is laid out in a grid pattern, with echoes of North American cities. Nathan Road, the main north–south downtown drag,

Above: A Volvo Olympian with Alexander bodywork dating from 1998, seen in service with Citybus on Hong Kong Island.

is a three-lane dual carriageway — a bit like Oxford Street on steroids.

So there's plenty of room for giant double-deckers, and plenty of need for them. And here they are, in massive profusion. The UK's buses seem almost diminutive by comparison.

Subjectively, you can't get away from the feeling that, in terms of quality, KMB is ahead of the game. Its low-floor air-conditioned fleet, now extensive, is finished in a livery of metallic gold that gives an irresistible air of elegance to the vehicles. I didn't see any bus with even the slightest hint of body damage at any time during my admittedly brief stay. And the impression is maintained inside. These vehicles feel more like coaches than buses.

Perhaps oddly, KMB has at least three liveries in current use. The air-conditioned non-low-floor buses are in a white livery, while the non-air-conditioned buses have a cream colour scheme. But even the oldest are smartly turned out.

The fleets on the island side have had a much shorter but perhaps more muddled history than KMB's and initially relied on a core of inherited or acquired vehicles. Buses in the Citybus fleet, wearing a mainly yellow livery reminiscent of Britain's own Bristol Citybus colour scheme of the 1980s, are well turned out but unmistakably older than their KMB counterparts. Those of New World First Bus are now generally

modern, but their livery doesn't match the elegant simplicity of KMB's, and their turnout is less consistent.

During British rule Hong Kong was a bastion of British-built double-decker buses. Ten years after Hong Kong was handed back to the Chinese you might wonder if the mix of vehicles would have changed to reflect a more international or even Eastern perspective.

The answer is yes and no. Yes, nowadays you'll see buses based on MAN, Neoplan and Scania chassis and bodies by Neoplan, Berkhof and Volgren, an Australian builder. But you can't help feeling that these have all been developed along British (or perhaps more correctly Hong Kong) lines. They still convey the ethos of the traditional double-decker.

In any case, the only emphatically 'non-British' models you'll see in any numbers at the moment are the 200-odd Neoplan Centroliners operated by KMB and New World, plus Volvo Super Olympians with Volgren bodywork. And the Volgren bodies look for all the world like recent models from some mysterious UK manufacturer, from Lancashire or Scotland, perhaps — one that no one told you about.

These apart, most of Hong Kong's recent buses are from Volvo and Alexander Dennis. Admittedly, the Volvo B9TL chassis are built in Poland. Can you consider an Australian-bodied Polish bus from a Swedish chassis manufacturer to be British in any sense? Perhaps it's all a question of perception.

What you won't find, sadly, are some of the buses that were once such a feature of the place. There are no more Guys, of course; nor any of the front-engined

Right: This Dennis Condor/Duple Metsec of New World First Bus was new to CMB in 1996, when it was rated to seat 103 passengers.

Left: Evoking an earlier era of public transport in Hong Kong is this 11m KMB Dennis Dragon, with its narrow entrance door, its sliding windows (no air conditioning) and its three-plus-two seating. The capacity is shown as 110 seated plus 43 standing.

Right: A Volvo Olympian with 91-seat Alexander bodywork. The smooth frontal styling of the Royale body is much more in evidence in Hong Kong than it ever was in the UK.

Dennis Jubilants that were created to replace them. You won't even see the three-axle Metrobuses that were such a feature of the Hong Kong landscape until quite recently and are now familiar on the London tourist trail.

You'll see little evidence either of the three-plus-two seating that until comparatively recently was widely used to increase capacity, and which partly accounts for the short-wheelbase three-axle models still in use. Bus travel Hong Kong-style is a bit less intensive nowadays.

What you *will* still see are plenty of Dennis Dragons (the three-axle version of the Dominator) and Dennis Condors (the version built for China Motor Bus). And plenty of Volvo Olympians, as well as some of the earlier Leyland version.

You'll also see a lot of angular Duple Metsec bodywork assembled from knocked-down kits, as well as a more recent Metsec body design, the DM5000, which is carried by many of the low-floor buses in several of the fleets. Its rounded contours give it a distinctly modern feel. Sadly, if you prize variety, there won't be any more of these, since production by latter-day owner TransBus was discontinued in 2002.

And alongside these, there are literally hundreds of familiar-looking Dennis and Volvo buses with Alexander ALX500 and R-type bodies, while KMB also has many Volvos with Wright Eclipse Gemini bodies.

As with buses in many parts of the world, things here are not always as they seem. Some Citybus vehicles that seem to have unmistakable Alexander R-type bodywork were actually bodied by Metsec but given Alexander front ends. And buses badged as Enviro500 are not necessarily based on Dennis chassis; they all carry the same Enviro branding, whether they are built on Dennis or Volvo B9TL chassis. Fortunately chassis manufacturers' badges make them easier to distinguish.

Is it just me, or is the Enviro500 bodywork more elegant than the Enviro400 supplied to UK operators? It looks as though it's based on the Northern Counties/

Below: The bus station at the Star Ferry terminal in Kowloon has a 1950s feel but is immaculately maintained. This is a KMB Neoplan Centroliner, seen against a backdrop of skyscrapers across the harbour on Hong Kong Island.

Plaxton President design, with a bit of added panache about the front end; and arguably the result is more stately somehow than that of the fussy and curvaceous 400. The Americans also get the 500 body style, and so do the Irish, but apparently not the Brits.

Will less conspicuously British products eventually change the status quo here? Not if Alexander Dennis has anything to do with it. Walking the streets here, you realise just what a fundamental role Hong Kong has played — and continues to play — in the company's emergence as Britain's leading bus manufacturer.

But the rest of the bus-building world won't stop looking for opportunities here. In 2007/8 KMB took delivery of a pair of Scania K310UD double-deckers

with bodywork by Caetano. This could be a sign of things to come, though I read that Citybus has chosen Enviro500s for its first batch of truly modern double-deckers.

A visit lasting just a few days isn't long enough to get the full measure of this extraordinary transport system. There are too many instances of photo opportunities just missed (a Berkhof-bodied MAN double-decker, for instance, or the unique Volgren prototype with Alexander-lookalike bodywork). There's so much more to see.

But it's long enough to be bowled over by the sheer intensity of the transport system, and by the realisation that until you've been here you simply haven't fully understood the point of double-decker buses. If you thought Oxford Street in rush hour was the epitome of high-density bus operation, you ain't seen nothin' yet. Go to Hong Kong, and let it change your perceptions forever.

I hear they have double-deckers in Singapore too …

Below: Contrary to appearances this Dennis Dragon, at the Star Ferry terminal on Hong Kong Island, has Duple Metsec bodywork with an Alexander R-type front end. It is one of a batch new to Citybus, finished by Caetano of Portugal.

Right: A KMB Dennis Trident with Alexander ALX500 bodywork against a sea of Chinese signs.

Left: New World First Bus also operates Neoplan Centroliner double-deckers.

Right: Among the smartest modern buses in the KMB fleet are these Alexander Dennis Enviro500s. This one is based on a Volvo B9TL chassis and has badging for both manufacturers. It is followed by the predecessor model, a Volvo B10TL 'Super Olympian', appropriately with the earlier Alexander ALX500 bodywork.

Right: An Alexander Dennis Enviro500 based on a Dennis chassis. Some KMB buses to this design carry Dennis badging.

Left: A Volgren-bodied Volvo B10TL in the KMB fleet at the pierside on Hong Kong Island.

Right: Seen in Nathan Road, Kowloon, this Scania N113 with Alexander RH bodywork is numerically the first of two prototypes bought experimentally by KMB in 1993 to trial 'cleaner' engines. An order for 20 followed.

Above: The last gasp of the Duple Metsec body range was the DM5000, here seen on Dennis Trident chassis in Kowloon.

Below: Hongkong Tramways has been around since 1904 and today operates the world's biggest fleet of double-deck tramcars — 163 — in regular public service. (The only others are in Blackpool and in Alexandria, Egypt.) This tram is one of a new type introduced in 2000.

Rolling stones

Robert E. Jowitt studies transport for the Isle of Wight Rock Festival ... not least from the bus-driver's seat.

"Someone always hits that stone!" said one of the regular drivers.

"What stone?" asked another.

Several regular drivers were in a huddle of conversation, as regular bus drivers tend to be in the presence of part-timers or interlopers from alien companies.

"That big white stone ... on the verge when you turn left out of the gate ..."

"Oh, *that* stone! Yes, someone always hits it ..."

Well, there had been only five sessions previous to this annual weekend revelry in which anyone could have hit it, but what the chaps said was probably true. Whether they were saying this as a friendly warning to me, a part-timer, or whether they did not care that I was listening and were simply gossiping, I do not know.

I decided, nevertheless, that I would not be among those who hit the stone ...

This conversation took place at the 2007 Isle of Wight Rock Festival, where, as part-time bus driver (if rather out of practice), I found myself suddenly included in this role.

The Isle of Wight Rock Festival had for many years been in point of fact a matter of ancient history, starting in flower-power days along with the likes of Glastonbury. From small beginnings a couple of years earlier it reached a magnificent apogee in 1970, with Joan Baez and other notables, and straining the ferry services and the Southern Vectis buses to their utmost limits. All I knew of it at the time was that as I was heading north from the New Forest in my lately acquired 1935 Parisian Renault bus to attend the Extravaganza at Crich we passed a constant string of Isle of Wight-bound hippy vehicles whose denizens invariably cheered and waved at the encounter.

Suffice it to say that the event seemed like an unrepeatable once-and-for-all, and nothing more was heard of it.

Only then, two or three years after the millennium, someone decided to revive the Isle of Wight Rock Festival.

Now let me state plainly here that anything I may say about the events which followed hereinafter might be largely based on hearsay and unsubstantiated myth, apart from such details as I myself encountered, and the reader must accept them as such. Anyway, myth and associated accounts are surely vital in the forming of legends ... For the sake of not adding what may be, perchance, not quite the truth, I will hereinafter append [myth?] to any comment I may make which could possibly fall into such category.

I set down the following experiences which I suffered or enjoyed simply from the bus-driver's point of view, along with a few observations from mayhem in the previous couple of years.

The original revival, in the year 2002, is alleged [myth?] to have been sponsored by the Isle of Wight Council or its Tourist Department or some such; and I, along with the rest of the Isle of Wight ratepayers, must have had to subsidise a fairly serious loss. An imaginative revival appeared almost total disaster.

SOUTHERN VECTIS
the island's buses 39155
Festival SINGLE
valid only Thursday 7th - Monday 11th June
2007

Left: One of the older vehicles involved in Festival transport in 2007 — but one which, to his regret, the author never managed to drive — was this former London Transport Leyland Titan of Emsworth & District. The stone which could catch unwary drivers leaving the Festival site is on the left.
Gordon Wigmore

Right: The newest buses in the Southern Vectis fleet, Mercedes-Benz Citaros, made their first operational journeys on the Festival service. Note the very tight squeeze past the post ... and bear in mind the post which you cannot see on the opposite side of the bus is just as close. *Gordon Wigmore*

Left: Festival contrast. On the left a Volvo Olympian from the London General fleet, and on the right Southern Vectis's venerable Bristol K. Both operators are part of Go-Ahead Group. *Ian Murray*

Nevertheless someone must have had faith in the restoration notion, and, moreover, for repeat performances, for 2003 and the next three years, found a sponsor. Thus the affair became known as the Nokia Festival. I must admit to being entirely naïve and unworldly in the machinations of sponsorship, though I am aware that the Isle of Wight is regarded as a healthy resort for such ploys.

Of Nokia I know little, save only the name is associated with mobile phones, such devices as I use only in extreme emotional or family-transport 'logistics', and one mobile phone to me is no different from another. My children tell me mine is effectively of dinosaur age ... but it works well enough.

It was in the Nokia era, while I was acting as custodian at the Isle of Wight Bus Museum on

Newport Quay, that, upon arriving for my turn of duty, I found the premises surrounded by heavy-metal fencing and equally heavy guards; the Museum was in close propinquity to the Festival-over-taken hotel and the general scene of operations.

The organisers promised that museum visitors would be allowed access; if I recall aright, *one* visitor braved the fences and guards. And isolated though we were at the Museum, we were afforded a grandstand seat for diverse aspects of musical transport, huge articulated lorries, often with foreign registration plates, and a vast three-axle double-deck bus, in silver and with occluded windows, which was, the guards said, the temporary mobile home of ... No, I forget entirely the name, having been long since out of touch with such names, but someone pretty famous anyway ...

From other Museum members I heard tell of (and on the fringes witnessed myself) the totally disruptive traffic measures employed for the occasion. And was perhaps a bit sorry I hadn't had the chance to go out and inspect the scene for myself …

Here, dear reader, please allow a little Island geography. The 1970 Festival had been held on empty farmland in West Wight; the revival was staged in the suburbs of the Island capital Newport. Someone somewhere was far-sighted enough to instigate a road scheme which, if far from pretty or adequate, served the purpose well enough and has remained in principle ever since …

It will be apparent that on the western side of the parallelogram, from the main 'bus-station-entrance' to the site, the traffic moves only south-westwards, with the other half of the road 'coned-off' as pedestrian space for the ravers to gain access to the supermarkets — and beer dispensers — of Newport. And back … if they don't choose to return to the Festival by using the shuttle-bus service from Newport, which fetches a five-mile circuit along the other sides of the parallelogram.

The residents of immediately-ill-affected suburbs either wrote letters of horror to the local press or indulged in 'off-road' sales of refreshment to the punters.

By my seclusion in the Bus Museum, and feeling, as I say, that I might have been missing something — not musically but bus-wise — I set forth on foot from Newport, on the last day of the Festival in 2006, along the one-way-busway/ two-way-pedestrian strip. As a student of humanity and fashion I feel bound to say that I have seldom if ever beheld a more hideously — sometimes scantily — attired procession, if always

cheerful, sometimes perhaps too much so! And with this two-way surge were one-way buses, where now and then I could greet a driver of my acquaintance to exchange derogatory comments on the scenario. Little then thought I of where I would be a year hence …

I arrived at last at the famous 'bus station', which, in a common agricultural field, proved to be a huge arrangement of metal sheets stretched out in something like D-Day style, all hemmed around with crash-barriers, many as queue-dividers in zigzag formation. To enter this the buses passed a frontier-type barrier, which some luckless employee had to raise for every passage. On leaving they passed another similar barrier and another luckless employee. After this they had to pass between two gateposts, fit for normal agricultural traffic but very tight for a constant string of buses, as I was to discover a year later, though I am pleased to record that I always squeezed through without damage. I would have thought that for minimal expense compared with what the 'bus station' must have cost they could have temporarily dug up one of these posts … and, by the same token, rolled the white stone away.

Naturally, being me, I took my photographic fill of this and then, except that I chose to toss an example of the proceeds therefrom into my next contribution for *Buses Yearbook 2008*, and described how, therein, I obtained what was the first and possibly the only senior-citizen ticket acquired during the Festival, I thought no more of the matter…

Only then, a year later, I was called up by a Southern Vectis chum who knew I held a PSV licence (or should I say now PCV?) to lend my weight to the effort. I couldn't really resist it, could I?

Right: The bus station at the Festival site was made up of heavy steel plates, to ensure buses had a solid surface to support them if the weather turned wet. Recently transferred to Southern Vectis from fellow Go-Ahead subsidiary Wilts & Dorset (which company's livery it still retained), this ECW-bodied Leyland Olympian had been new to Crosville in 1984. *Ian Murray*

Right: Going down to the Festival, but with only one passenger, an open-top Bristol VRT from the Southern Vectis fleet. It was new in 1980 with a V-suffix registration. *Ian Murray*

Below: Appropriate message on the back of a Mecedes-Benz Citaro. *Ian Murray*

Right: Well, no question what this area is intended for. A London General Routemaster emerges from incongruous surroundings. *Ian Murray*

Right: An Ulster registration disguises the age of this Southern Vectis Leyland Olympian, although those with sharp eyes might spot that it has a Workington-built Leyland body rather than an ECW body — which reduces the options. It dates from 1989, and the registration matches its fleet number. It was originally F711 SDL.
Ian Murray

This next, in June 2007, claimed [myth?] to be host to 50,000 fans. Some people say there may have been 100,000. There were certainly ticket scams … some of them caught out! Note that the population of the Island is about 150,000 …

I was booked on for five days, the first two to be spent in selling tickets at the Ferry Terminal at Fishbourne, to such addicts as chose that point of arrival. The further three days were to be spent driving as and when and where required.

Now Fishbourne is a jolly little place full of elite residents whose only complaint, apart from the prospect of being drowned in the next 50 years through global warming, is the disorder of the Wightlink car ferry.

Myself and another chap, by his own admission once a student of agricultural college but later hooked by Go-Ahead Group for bus enterprise — and be it remembered that by this date (which hadn't applied to previous festivals) Southern Vectis was now part of that elite title — did our best to sell tickets to the 'foot-passengers'. We did so with the aid of a horrid Ford Transit van to serve as ticket office and a hired tough Polish security guard to kill anyone who tried to rob us or the Transit … or the sandwiches and Coke which Southern Vectis now and then supplied.

Deeming that enough was enough, the agricultural student departed to try his hand at driving RMLs or whatever else offered. Even Robert E. Jowitt, alone, could cope with the half-hourly influx of ticket-selling,

Left: Another Go-Ahead subsidiary, Metrobus, provided this handsome RML-type Routemaster in London Transport Country Area livery — which seems particularly apt for the rural Isle of Wight. *Ian Murray*

Left: A Stagecoach tri-axle Olympian in South West Trains livery arrives from the mainland. This Alexander-bodied bus was new to Citybus in Hong Kong. *Ian Murray*

Right: A one-time City of Cardiff Bristol VRT/Alexander stirs up the dust as it pulls out of the Festival grounds. New in 1979 as a convertible, it was by now part of the Solent Blue Line fleet. *Ian Murray*

while the tough from Poland (his name was Roland) helpfully heaved baggage and rolled-up tents into the boots of the coaches.

The coaches, though admittedly quite smart and pretty, were actually two derelicts from the Oxford Express [myth?] about to be transferred elsewhere, if not to the scrap-heap, which were driven now and then by a drafted-in Go-Ahead manager with whom I was to some extent acquainted and a very pleasant lady who usually drove buses in Hythe (South Hants), or somewhere like that.

The second day of this commitment was more tedious than the first. While many incoming motor cars, stuffed with tents and hippies almost like those of 1970, rolled past a huge press of outgoing cars — presumably Islanders fleeing the turmoil — they so completely jammed the loading bays that there was no room for our coaches to turn around and reach their designated stop.

Then thereafter, the next day, I was chucked into whatever might be needed in driving for the affray … and of course, missing the stone!

My recollections thereafter may be somewhat dim. In my first moments, trying to explain to anyone who might be in a responsible position and able to help that it was quite a while since I had handled an automatic or even semi-automatic gear and might need a bit of reminding about the finer points … "Yeah, he's a bus driving instructor, if you ain't familiar with the vehicle he'll tell you what to do …" All this on the back of an RML roaring joyously up to the site.

Our bus instructor put me onto a Volvo, by name *New Ditch Point*. He accompanied me on the run back into Newport and, with a "Yes, will you be okay now?", departed upon matters of doubtless more pressing urgency, hardly waiting for a reply… but I thought I would probably be okay. I mean, it isn't really very difficult. Southern Vectis has the delightful habit of furnishing its buses with names, derived in the main from coastal locations on the Island, but I have to admit that, even as a serious student of OS maps, I have never discovered the whereabouts of said New Ditch. To this I might add that, to the best of my recollection, having been brought up in Herefordshire single-deck territory, this was in all probability the first double-decker I ever drove. No problem!

I wish I could have kept her!

Exigencies in the scene demanded, over the next two or three days, that I must try my luck on Heaven knows what.

I have been told that 38 extra buses from 'abroad' were drafted in for 2007, quite apart from such regular IoW buses as might be available, this number having been slowly augmented since the first days of 2002, when Island-based buses proved adequate to cope with almost-a-flop.

At some stage Southern Vectis introduced the sensible habit of allocating visiting buses with temporary fleet numbers, this apparently primarily for recording fuel consumption. In the early years of the millennium these hardly reached double figures — or perhaps less — but in 2006 we had fleet numbers 1400-30, and by 2007 we were on to 1501-38. These numbers, at least in 2007 — and I can't say I noticed before then — were affixed as little self-adhesive discs to front and rear of the buses, in a yellowy-orange. As I was always fascinated (see *Buses Yearbook 1989*) by the poetry or sometimes symmetry of bus numbers, fleet or route or operational, I was rather charmed by this.

At one point in the frenzy I was directed to take out the Alexander Dennis demonstrator — or whatever it was — and while I gazed somewhat distraught in the driving-seat at a dashboard like enough to a Dan Dare space-ship I was, somewhat to my relief, called off to handle something else instead.

Several weeks later I chanced to encounter again this demonstrator, an Enviro400, at a vehicle rally at Redhill, Surrey, and the creature was still proudly boasting its IoW Festival number. Moreover, I seem to recall that in streets around Portsmouth or the South Coast, in other subsequent weeks, I sighted other of those yellowy-orange discs. After all, whose business was it to remove them? For someone in Emsworth, for example, they might think to let well alone and not

A Northern Counties-bodied Volvo Olympian in the Southern Vectis fleet awaits Festival-goers. *Ian Murray*

destroy vital evidence. For all I know some of those discs may be around still.

From Dennis I was bidden onto a K-reg Southern Vectis Leyland, only to be evicted with "This one's mine! It's always mine!" … and then I had some nasty little Wilts & Dorset Optares and a couple of Wiltax double-deckers. One of these was a delightfully responsive gem, the other was passing dreadful.

At this stage of the proceedings we were still engaged primarily in Festival–Newport traffic and, in quiet moments, were well fed by ladies attached to SV busy with barbecues and so forth, and I think I must record that a delightful 'family atmosphere' was prevalent among all who could enjoy a few minutes' respite in that tin-plated bus terminal. Eventually, however, the terminal started to suffer, and all who were available around the barbecue were summoned

to stand on one of the tin-plates so that a bus which had become bogged in by the shifting of the plates could actually move on and out. Health & Safety regulations were at naught, the plate heaved a bit despite the weight, but the bus moved on …

The last act of the Festival was the Rolling Stones.

Now here we go back to antiquity. I, once, attended a Rolling Stones concert at the Gaumont, Bournemouth, performed totally dead-pan, never a smile, 'I used to love her but it's all over now', the obligatory rush by screaming teenage girls gently repressed by paternal policemen, and exit to street still graced by Sunbeam MF2B trolleybuses. Moreover my sister, travelling on train, Southern Region, still steam-hauled, 'Merchant Navy' or other of Bulleid ilk, found herself in the corridor next to the compartment occupied by the Rolling Stones. She tried to obtain their autographs,

Left: New and old. The Enviro400 demonstrator — which the author almost drove — dwarfs the Southern Vectis Bristol behind it. Buses have become bigger over the 70 years separating the two designs.
The demonstrator carries a temporary fleet number in the windscreen.
Ian Murray

Right: The borrowed Wilts & Dorset MetroRiders did not endear themselves to Robert Jowitt, who cuttingly describes them as 'nasty little Optares'. This bus had been new to Trent in 1996. *Ian Murray*

was told quietly *no.* She thinks Mick Jagger himself may have said it; anyway, they were all too tired.

Forty years on, the Rolling Stones being booked for revival as the final act for the IoW Festival, my sister, not inclined to buy a ticket, went, like hundreds of other IoW residents, to hear the concert from the opposite side of the River Medina (which flanks the Festival site). She (as a classical musician) wonders if they weren't half a tone out.

I had already quit the scene, to come back on the morrow to attend to residual operations. Meanwhile the Rolling Stones, with what was said to be a convoy of 60 vehicles [myth?], many of them buses or coaches, had chartered the entirety of the Yarmouth–Lymington Ferry to ship same back to Old England's shores. Actually there is no way you could fit 60 coaches onto a Yarmouth–Lymington ferry, but the reaction of Festival visitants who had thought they might catch that ferry, still apparently timetabled [myth?], was not favourable to the Rolling Stones.

The most striking feature of the last day, the day of abandonment, was the huge number of tents left behind by the Festi-campers, all of which were trashed and smashed by the guys clearing the site. I will not dwell on the ecological or financial waste of such wanton destruction. I was, as before, hither and thither, and by the time I had picked up a bus and brought it back, via the circuit of the tin-plates, to where I thought it ought to be, I was told I was going somewhere else instead. I think I went to East Cowes once, West Cowes once too; perhaps even Ryde, with one bus or another, and full of Festi-punters.

Left: This Leyland Titan, heading underneath the camping arch, was one of the few supplied new outside London — in this case to Reading Transport. Surrey-based Wiltax was purchased by Tellings Golden Miller in July 2007. *Ian Murray*

Right: The South West Trains livery is brighter than Stagecoach's standard bus colour scheme, as this view of the hired Olympian shows. Any Scottish Festival-goers who were heading home and saw a bus proclaiming 'Glasgow' as its destination must have thought it was their lucky day. *Ian Murray*

Vehicles hired for the 2007 Festival (table compiled by Richard Newman)

1501	R809 NUD	Volvo B10M/Plaxton	Oxford Bus Company (70)
1502	R401 DWL	Volvo B10M/Plaxton	Oxford Bus Company (8)
1503	P240 CTV	Optare MetroRider	Wilts & Dorset (2240)
1504	R402 DWL	Volvo B10M/Plaxton	Oxford Bus Company (11)
1505	R810 NUD	Volvo B10M/Plaxton	Oxford Bus Company (69)
1506	LYR 910	AEC Regent III/Park Royal	Greene Lane (RT3491)
1507	469 CLT	AEC/Park Royal Routemaster	Greene Lane (RMC1469)
1508	P238 CTV	Optare MetroRider	Wilts & Dorset (2238)
1509	M537 JLJ	Optare MetroRider	Wilts & Dorset (2537)
1510	M536 JLJ	Optare MetroRider	Wilts & Dorset (2536)
1511	A883 SUL	Leyland Titan	Emsworth & District
1512	UFX 857S	Bristol VRT/ECW open-top	Solent Blue Line (901)
1513	C436 BUV	MCW Metrobus	Wiltax, New Haw
1514	R362 LGH	Volvo Olympian/Northern Counties	London General (NV162)
1515	SK07 DYB	Alexander Dennis Enviro400	Alexander Dennis (demonstrator)
1516	WLT 516	AEC/Park Royal Routemaster	London General (RML2516)
1517	JJD 520D	AEC/Park Royal Routemaster	London General (RML2520)
1518	R373 LGH	Volvo Olympian/Northern Counties	London General (NV173)
1519	WTG 360T	Bristol VRT/Alexander open-top	Solent Blue Line (902)
1520	YJB 68T	Leyland Titan/Park Royal	Wiltax, New Haw
1521	M746 RCP	DAF SB3000/Van Hool	Damory Coaches (5014)
1522	M574 RCP	DAF SB3000/Van Hool	Damory Coaches (5013)
1523	R832 MFR	Volvo Olympian/East Lancs	Metrobus (832)
1524	CUV 317C	AEC/Park Royal Routemaster	Metrobus (RML2317)
(1525-8 non-PSVs)			
1529	H463 EJR	Leyland Olympian/Alexander	Stagecoach (13646)
1530	OUC 45R	Leyland Fleetline/Metro-Cammell	Emsworth & District
(1531 non-PSV)			
1532	H764 KDY	Leyland Olympian/Alexander	Stagecoach (13634)
1533	H462 EJR	Leyland Olympian/Alexander	Stagecoach (13652)
1534	T216 REL	DAF SB3000/Plaxton	Wilts & Dorset (3216)
1535	YJ05 PXN	VDL DB250/East Lancs	Marchwood Motorways
1536	J205 VHN	DAF SB220/Optare Delta	Southern Transit, Brighton
1537	P228 CTV	Optare MetroRider	Wilts & Dorset (2238)
1538	TJI 7520	Leyland Tiger/Plaxton	Kardan Travel, Newport

The traffic jams were still dreadful: I can see yet the vision of maybe a mile ahead of me, both lanes entirely full of cars and buses, perhaps six buses either way. This may be nothing in Birmingham or London, but by my own Isle of Wight standards it is an impressive if slightly depressing spectacle.

And the stone? Let me just add that one driver, of course an interloper, managed, when probably dead tired after a long day and perchance momentarily distracted by drunken idiots near the gate, not only to hit that damned white stone and buckle the nearside bottom flank of an SV Volvo (*Watcombe Bay*, or some other place unknown on the map) but also to roll the stone many inches from its proper resting-place.

Anonymity must here prevail.

From White Ladies to Black Witches

Few bus routes have retained a recognisable identity for more than half a century. **Roy Marshall** illustrates the X43, which connects East Lancashire with Manchester, showing vehicles covering six decades.

There has been a bus service from the Burnley area to Manchester since the 1920s, and for most of that time it has been operated by Ribble as the X43, starting in Colne and for a time even offering journeys from Skipton.

In recent years the service has been cut back to start at Nelson — partly because of low passenger numbers between Nelson and Colne, and partly to reduce the length of the route to avoid drivers being subject to EU hours rules.

The X43 made use of the new M66 motorway when it opened in 1978, bypassing the Bury to Edenfield section of the original route. Buses remained on that route, adopting the number 743. The motorway cut the journey time to Manchester, which led to increased passenger numbers and improved frequencies.

After the privatisation of the National Bus Company, Ribble — initially the subject of a management buy-out — was taken over by Stagecoach. Then, in 2001, Ribble's Burnley-area operations were acquired by Blazefield, trading as Burnley & Pendle, and the new company took on the X43. Today Burnley & Pendle is owned by French company Transdev.

Below: Operating on the X43 in 1950 was this stylish Burlingham-bodied Leyland Titan PD1 in the Ribble fleet. It is seen in Manchester's Lower Moseley Street bus station. Known as 'White Ladies', 30 of these striking vehicles were purchased in 1948/9 for use on limited-stop services. A further 20, with East Lancs bodies on PD2 chassis, followed in 1950/1. This site is now occupied by the Bridgewater Hall.

Right: A late-1940s Burlingham-bodied Leyland Tiger, operating as a duplicate on the X43 on a busy Saturday in Skipton in August 1959. The scheduled bus was the Leyland Titan just visible behind the Tiger.

Left: More-modern vehicles used on the service at the end of the 1950s and early 1960s were Ribble's distinctive full-fronted Leyland Titan PD3s. This one, with Burlingham body, is loading in Skipton bus station, with a Tiger standing by in the background in case the Titan's 72 seats are not enough.

Right: Lower Moseley Street again, but now in 1966 and with a dual-purpose Weymann-bodied Leyland Leopard standing by to work an X43 to Burnley.

Left: From the 1970s 'proper' coaches were often used on the X43. A 1965 Plaxton-bodied Leopard in National coach livery enters Rawtenstall *en route* to Burnley in 1974.

Below: This is a 1982 view, showing a route-branded Leopard with Duple Dominant II body passing Burnley bus station on its way to Manchester. The branding includes the wording '*REGULAR MOTORWAY SERVICE*', acknowledging the recent opening of the M66. Burnley bus station is on the left of the picture.

Left: In 1984 four ECW-bodied Leyland Olympians were delivered to Ribble. Fitted with 70 high-backed seats and finished in a livery of white and two-tone blue, they were lettered '*TIMESAVER*', as the X43 was branded at this time. A new Olympian loads in Rawtenstall on its way to Manchester in June 1984.

Above: A new Timesaver livery of red and yellow was used on four Leyland Tigers with relatively rare Duple Laser 2 bodywork, delivered in 1985. They were 11m-long 49-seaters. This one is seen on the 743, which avoided the M66 and instead used the old road through Bury.

Left: Stagecoach bought Ribble in 1989, quickly applying its corporate livery. This is one of the 1984 Timesaver Olympians, at Colne in 1991.

Right: Under Stagecoach ownership Ribble introduced Plaxton Premieres to the X43, now branded the Mancunian. This 11m-long Dennis Javelin, seen in Burnley in 1994, was one of 20 47-seaters delivered the previous year. The wording 'TO & FROM MANCHESTER' appears below the destination display.

Above: For a short time the X43 was operated in part by Stagecoach's Volvo B10M artics. Four were allocated to the X43 in 1996, but their use was short-lived. Parked cars and restrictions on their use in Bury bus station and in Rawtenstall saw them transferred elsewhere within the Stagecoach group. This coach has a 71-seat Plaxton Premiere body.

Left: In 2001 Blazefield took over Stagecoach's Burnley business. Still in Stagecoach livery, this ex-Burnley & Pendle Volvo Citybus sports the revived Burnley & Pendle name, visible above the driver's side window. New in 1991, the bus, with an 82-seat Alexander R-type body, is seen arriving in Colne 10 years later, its dot-matrix destination already set for the return trip to Manchester.

Right: Also seen in 2001 is a one-time Highland Omnibuses Leyland Olympian, new in 1983, getting ready for service in Burnley bus station for a peak-hour trip to Manchester. Like the Citybus it carries the new Burnley & Pendle name. It has the low-height version of Alexander's R-type body, with 77 bus seats.

Right: Blazefield revitalised the X43 in 2001 with a fleet of 15 new Volvo B7TLs with coach-seated Plaxton President bodies. They were 71-seaters. This one, pictured in 2005, is leaving Burnley for the Trafford Centre, south of Manchester, operating as an X42. The extension of the service to the Trafford Centre was short-lived. The route branding introduced a witch, located above the first side window on the lower deck.

Above: In 2005 the X43 was again upgraded with a further 15 new B7TLs with high-specification 68-seat Wright Eclipse Gemini bodies and a new livery and name: The Witch Way. The buses were named after local witches; *Anne Redfearne* is seen passing Burnley's impressive town hall, completed in 1888. The black livery was first used by Blazefield on similar buses operating between Harrogate and Leeds.

The Witch Way

User Guide
Fourth Edition
29 July 2007

LCC Leaflet No. 62

X43 X44
Nelson
Burnley
Rawtenstall
Edenfield
M66
Prestwich
Manchester

Tel: Burnley (01282) 427778
www.thewitchway.co.uk

From Poppy to Barbie

David Cole looks at the wide variety of vehicles operated by Midland Red (West) since its creation in 1981.

The name 'Midland Red' was once synonymous with travel through a vast swathe of central England. Loved or loathed by its passengers, it was their principal mode of travel for several generations. Yet today there are few direct traces of what was once Britain's largest provincial bus company. Privatised and regrouped, its successors still provide quality services on many routes with their origins in Midland Red, but the buses will be any colour but red.

One of those successors retained a red-based livery and 'Midland Red' in its fleetname and publicity for longer than the others. This was Midland Red (West) Ltd, which later traded as First Midland Red — a name removed from late 2001, when First adopted a single national brand for its bus services. At that time almost all First Midland Red buses were still in red livery, the legacy of having a modern fleet of step-entrance buses which did not qualify for the group's corporate 'Barbie' livery, which was initially applied only to low-floor buses with the group's standard interior trim. Unlike most other First subsidiaries, it had been allocated no new buses in the original 'Barbie' livery style, and even the revised 'Barbie 2' style was slow to appear, the first vehicles so adorned being minibuses transferred from First Eastern Counties earlier in 2001.

The start of Midland Red's demise can be traced back to the late 1950s when passenger numbers started to decline, a trend accelerated by the withdrawal of non-remunerative parts of the network and the loss of scheduled services through staff and vehicle shortages. The dense network of routes in Birmingham and the Black Country which had generated much of the company's profits were sold to the West Midlands PTE in 1973. Whilst this benefited passengers in those areas through the integration of services, it left the remainder of the company significantly dependent on local-authority subsidies to maintain its operations.

Midland Red now had a Polo-shaped operating area and oversized headquarters functions despite a series of acquisitions, so it is perhaps surprising that the division of the business into smaller units by the National Bus Company did not take place until 1981.

Six units were created. There were four geographical bus companies — North, East, South and West — whose territory is now covered by three of the major groups. Arriva covers what were North and East, Stagecoach covers South, while First operates in the West area. There was also a coach company, which passed into Midland Red (West) ownership at privatisation, and an engineering company, the remnants of the old Birmingham & Midland Motor Omnibus Co workshops, based on the central works in Carlyle Road, Birmingham. Part of the latter operation, relocated and re-branded as Carlyle, survives today, offering parts and service to bus and coach operators.

A feature of the new companies was the use of legal and secretarial services of adjacent NBC units. In the case of Midland Red (West) these services were provided by Bristol Omnibus, and the company's registered address was in Bristol rather than at its own headquarters in Edgar Street, Worcester.

At its inception on 6 September 1981 Midland Red (West) inherited a relatively standardised fleet of 183 vehicles, comprising 121 Leyland Nationals, 60 Leyland Leopards and two Ford midibuses converted by Midland Red from full-size Plaxton Derwent-bodied R1014s.

A few all-over advertisements aside, NBC poppy red was the standard livery across the fleet. On Leyland Nationals there was normally a white relief band at roof level which carried the fleetname and the local identity. These were 'Severnlink' for Worcester and Bromsgrove, 'Wendaway' for Kidderminster, 'Wandaward' for Hereford and 'Reddibus' for Redditch. Most of the Leopards carried NBC's red-and-white dual-purpose livery. The fleetname '**MIDLAND RED WEST**', in standard NBC style, was applied from early 1982.

Within its first month of existence Midland Red (West) became embroiled in service revisions associated with the Hereford trial area, in which licensing conditions had been relaxed to assess the

Above: Poppy red was the livery used by Midland Red at the time of its division into four separate bus-operating companies. This was Midland Red's first Leyland National and typifies Midland Red (West)'s single-deck fleet in the 1980s. There were 121 Nationals in the fleet when the company was created in 1981.

Below: Looking rather the worse for wear, a 1972 Leyland Leopard with 53-seat Marshall body and 'Reddibus' branding ensures people know where it's going with a destination display reading 'REDDITCH Via Redditch'.

Left: This Daimler Fleetline was the first vehicle to be added to Midland Red (West)'s inherited fleet, being acquired from Trent in 1981 for additional school services in the Hereford trial area. In full NBC livery with 'Wandaward' local branding (but with 'WEST' yet to be added to the fleetname), it is seen in March 1982 working a normal daytime service.

impact of the Government's proposals for bus-service deregulation. Here new school contracts resulted in the acquisition, from Trent, of the company's first double-deckers, three J-registered Alexander-bodied Daimler Fleetlines; these lasted less than three years, gradually being swapped for Leyland Nationals from other Midland Red companies. A further Fleetline came from Midland Red South for a contract in Evesham in exchange for a Leopard coach, again only spending a short time in the fleet.

A more visible manifestation of the trial area was the introduction of a free bus in association with local operator Yeomans. For this a Willowbrook-bodied Leopard was painted yellow with fleetnames for both companies and 'FREE BUS' lettering. The latter was soon covered over as the vehicle moved to other

duties, and in April 1983 Midland Red (West) acquired Yeomans' share of the Hereford city services. An unexpected competitor appeared soon after, resulting in Midland Red (West)'s needing to hire in vehicles, two of which were Duple-bodied Bedford YMTs from Yeomans; in Yeomans livery with Midland Red (West) legal lettering and fleet numbers, these were used initially on Hereford services, later moving to Worcester, where they gained National white, both surviving in the fleet until the autumn of 1987.

There were a number of firsts for the company in 1983. These included the first (and only) articulated buses operated and the first new vehicle. The artics were five MANs which had been used by South Yorkshire PTE and arrived in January on a 12-month loan; used on the core 'Reddibus' circular services

Left: Acquired from Yeomans in 1983, this 1976 Bedford YMT with 53-seat Duple Dominant body was used initially on bus services in Hereford before migrating to coach duties. Still in Yeomans' livery when seen in April 1984 in Bromsgrove, it additionally displays **'MIDLAND RED WEST'** stickers, as well as both MRW (845) and Yeomans (3) fleet numbers.

in Redditch, they retained South Yorkshire PTE livery but with 'Reddibus' branding. The new vehicle, which arrived in the summer, was also the company's first true coach, a Leyland Tiger with Plaxton Paramount 3500 body in National white livery. In 1985 this would be the first vehicle to receive the new 'MidWest' coach livery of maroon and gold on a white base.

In conjunction with the other former Midland Red companies, a new livery was adopted in 1983 for the dual-purpose vehicles used on longer-distance services. Branded 'Midland Express', the red-and-yellow variation on the 'Venetian blind' livery popular at the time was applied mainly to the Plaxton Supreme-bodied Leopards (although a number of bus-seated

Top: Five MAN articulated buses were hired in 1983 for 'Reddibus' services. This former MAN demonstrator, still in its South Yorkshire PTE livery, is seen loading at one of the temporary stops in use while Redditch bus station was being rebuilt in April 1983.

Above: Midland Red (West)'s first new buses were six suburban-express Leyland National 2s finished in Midland Express livery. One arrives in Bromsgrove in April 1984 when brand-new.

Leyland Nationals would be so treated in 1986), as well as to the company's first new service buses — six Leyland National 2s to suburban-express specification, delivered in March 1984.

In 1983 one of the two Ford/Plaxton midibuses was upgraded to dual-purpose status and painted in National white, before gaining 'MidWest' livery in 1985. In that year the other Ford midibus conversion was further rebuilt, being equipped with a wheelchair lift.

A further coach (re)joined the fleet in March 1984. One of the company's two Willowbrook 003-bodied Leyland Leopards had been severely damaged in 1983 and was given a new Plaxton Paramount 3200 body and a new identity with an unusual Q-prefix registration (Q276 UOC), becoming one of the first PCVs to be so registered. In this form it was to remain in the fleet until 2001.

Overall, the fleet was fairly settled for the first four years of the company's existence. Withdrawals concentrated on the Leyland Leopards with bus-style dual-purpose bodies, their place being taken by a number of Plaxton- and Duple-bodied Leopards and assorted Leyland Nationals, the latter including early examples from Northern General and the very first Midland Red example, 101, which had passed initially to Midland Red (East). However, this situation was to change significantly in 1985, following the company's decision to adopt widespread minibus operation on its town and city networks.

The first new vehicles in 1985 were, however, more coaches, and in March and April there arrived six Leyland Tigers, this time with the lower 3200 version of Plaxton's Paramount body, two each in 'MidWest', National Express 'Rapide' and 'Eurocruising' liveries.

By October a number of minibuses were on hire for driver training at Worcester, ready for the city's new network to be launched on 23 November. This required 60 Mercedes-Benz L608D minibuses, which carried a distinctive yellow-and-blue livery and had had their van bodywork converted by three builders — Robin Hood (40), PMT (19) and Alexander (one). Many of these vehicles, which replaced just 18 Leyland Nationals, would achieve long lives, latterly in standard bus livery. Six were upgraded with coach seating within the first six months of operation, and one of these remained in service to 2001, believed to be the longest-lived of any first-generation minibus with its original operator. The Worcester fleet was augmented for three months early in 1986 by a demonstration Iveco with Robin Hood body.

A further 44 Mercedes-Benz L608Ds arrived early in 1986, 25 entering service at Kidderminster on 8 March on the Wyre Forest Shuttle in yellow and green, and 18 at Redditch on 19 April in 'Reddilink' yellow and red; the final vehicle joined the Worcester fleet. These vehicles had been converted for bus use by Robin Hood (21) and by a new supplier to the fleet, Reeve Burgess.

Below: Between November 1985 and April 1986 just over 100 Mercedes-Benz L608Ds joined the Midland Red (West) fleet. This 20-seater, with 'ReddiLink' branding, was converted by Robin Hood.

The new image presented by the minibus fleet was extended to the predominantly Leyland National bus fleet in mid-1986 with the application of a tasteful cream, red and black colour scheme with a fleetname in shaded lettering, accompanied by the company's new Wyvern logo.

In readiness for deregulation, the company unveiled proposals to base a fleet of Leyland Nationals at Digbeth, Birmingham, where it had recently assumed responsibility for maintenance of the National Express coach station. These were to be used on new local services in south-west Birmingham and on West Midlands PTE contracted services across the West Midlands.

Deregulation was implemented early in Hereford & Worcester, on 31 August 1986. Amongst other changes, Midland Red (West) lost a number of services around Bromsgrove to the PTE-owned West Midlands Travel. Together with vehicles retained following the introduction of the minibus networks, this provided Leyland Nationals for the Digbeth allocation, to which were added 22 second-hand examples from South Wales, Devon General, Ribble and Midland Red (North). A further seven had arrived from Midland Fox — the former Midland Red (East) — by the end of 1986, to be followed early in 1987 by four more plus some grant coaches from Midland Red (North).

Besides presenting the challenges of deregulation, 1986 marked the change of Midland Red (West)'s legal address from Bristol to London Road, Worcester, and ended with the company's privatisation on 23 December. This involved a management buy-out

which also included the 38-vehicle fleet of Midland Red Coaches, known previously as Midland Red (Express). This included two Mercedes-Benz minibuses, one of which was soon converted to dual-purpose specification and added to the 'ReddiLink' fleet.

The Midland Red Coaches name was used for coach operations until 1997, when most of the remaining coaches were sold, although in the interim many coaches had joined the bus fleet as dual-purpose vehicles, initially in the later, bolder version of Midland Express livery before gaining standard red and cream. These included another Plaxton Paramount-rebodied Leyland Leopard with a Q-prefix registration (Q553 UOC), giving the company the rare distinction of operating two Q-registered vehicles.

After all the changes of 1986, 1987 was a relatively quiet year on the vehicle front as the privatised company established itself in the deregulated environment. Management focus was also on growth, and this manifested itself in the purchase from NBC of Bristol Citybus. Very quickly, Bristol VRTs were loaned from Bristol to Redditch to match new competition from Redline, a business set up by former Midland Red employees to provide a double-deck service around the town. After a number of vehicle changes three VRTs were transferred to Midland Red (West)

Above: This Ford R1014 was one of a number shortened by Midland Red in 1978/9 to produce midibuses. Midland Red (West) later converted it to carry wheelchairs, with a lift and double opening doors just ahead of the rear wheel. Originally a 45-seater, it now provided seating for just 19. It is seen in Worcester in 1988.

ownership in April 1988, although these retained Bristol fleet numbers and livery with the addition of bold '**MIDLAND RED WEST**' fleetnames. Like the Trent Fleetlines in the early 1980s, the VRTs would be relatively short-lived, being withdrawn late in 1990.

The only new vehicles in 1987 were six Reeve Burgess-converted Mercedes-Benz minibuses, this time based on the 709D. Five were allocated to Kidderminster with 'Shuttle' branding; the sixth joined the 'Reddilink' fleet. The company also tried a number of demonstrators, including a Leyland Lynx and various minibuses.

After less than 18 months as a separate company Midland Red West Holdings merged with Badgerline Holdings on 26 April 1988, bringing Bristol city and country services back into a single group. Soon afterwards Badgerline was identified as a source of additional minibuses, no fewer than 17 Robin Hood-bodied Ivecos joining the Midland Red West operation (most retaining their previous liveries), whilst a Mercedes minibus came from Bristol to join the 'Shuttle' fleet at Kidderminster. In the meantime further deliveries of new Mercedes-Benz 709Ds, converted by Reeve Burgess, enabled Hereford city services to be converted to minibus operation on 23 April 1988. This required 28 vehicles, of which 26 were delivered in a green-and-yellow livery, the last two arriving in plain white in readiness for the application of all over advertisements. The Hereford minibuses carried names, mainly recalling famous local characters,

although some were rather whimsical, such as 'On and Offa'!

Nine second-hand Mercedes-Benz minibuses provided the only significant change to the fleet in 1989. These came from Southdown, one becoming a 'Shuttle' at Kidderminster, the rest augmenting the fleet at Worcester, where one was given a special livery to celebrate the 800th anniversary of the city's charter. On the debit side, the dual-purpose National 2s of 1984, some of which had latterly worn the revised style of Midland Express livery, left the fleet for Badgerline, along with the two earlier Leyland National 2s inherited from the original Midland Red company. During the same year Leyland National 101 became a yellow-liveried driver-training vehicle, a status it was to retain until restored to original red livery for the centenary of Midland Red in 2004.

The renewal of the full-size single-deck fleet, composed largely of Leyland Nationals by now between 10 and 15 years old, commenced in 1990. The first arrivals were more Nationals, three later models from Western National, but these were upstaged in April by the largest single batch of full-size vehicles to join the fleet. Following trials of various demonstrators the Leyland Lynx was chosen for 50 vehicles — 42 to renew the fleet operating in the West Midlands from Digbeth, the remainder to provide an upgrade on the principal routes in Redditch.

The other new vehicles in 1990 introduced a new make, the Talbot Pullman, a three-axle easy-access minibus chosen following use earlier in the year of a demonstrator and a comparison trial with a CVE Omni. The seven Pullmans were delivered in the West Midlands PTE's green-and-yellow 'Quickstep' livery for tendered services.

Four more second-hand Mercedes-Benz L608Ds arrived about the same time, these coming from Brighton & Hove. They were the first minibuses in the standard red-and-cream livery, which was now applied to all minibuses due for repainting, eliminating the local liveries, although local identities were retained, while in 1992, to commemorate the 350th anniversary of the start of the Civil War, 12 of Worcester minibuses were given names recalling the city's role in that conflict.

The new-vehicle intake of 1990 spelled the end for many Leyland Nationals, including the last example still in NBC-style poppy red, and also the last bus-shell Leyland Leopard dual-purpose vehicles.

During 1992 and 1993 the ranks of the older Leopard/Plaxton grant coaches were thinned, some replacement being effected by downgrading vehicles from the Midland Red Coaches fleet.

The next arrival of vehicles from an outside source was not until late 1993, when 11 Reeve Burgess-converted Mercedes-Benz L608Ds arrived from Bristol to replace most of the Ivecos still in stock.

A further significant investment in the Birmingham and Black Country operation was made in the spring of 1994 with the delivery of 37 Plaxton Verde-bodied Dennis Lances, this combination representing the Badgerline group's standard full-size single-decker. These replaced the Digbeth Lynxes (which now migrated to Redditch or Kidderminster), although their stay was short. Around a year after their introduction a reorganisation took bus operations out of Digbeth, the Lances moving to other depots, although some

Below: Hereford city services were converted to minibus operation in April 1988 using Mercedes' updated 609D model. This 20-seater, a Reeve Burgess conversion, is seen the following month in the city centre. It is named *The Saracen*, the name being displayed above the entrance.

Left: The first Plaxton Verde-bodied Dennis Lances entered service on Birmingham and Black Country routes in March 1994. Just a few days old, one is seen in Dudley bus station surrounded by Metrowest Leyland Nationals. The badger behind the rear wheel was the Badgerline group's corporate logo.

Right: Of the batch of 50 Leyland Lynxes delivered in 1990 all congregated eventually at Redditch, where many would remain into 'Barbie' days. The short-lived Midland Red West fleetname in FirstBus corporate style is seen on this bus in Birmingham's Bristol Road *en route* to its home town in October 1997.

remained outstationed at Birmingham's (by now largely deserted) Bull Ring bus station. A second batch of 19 Lances, differing only in minor details, arrived in the summer of 1995 for the trunk routes out of Worcester. The arrival of the Lances spelled the end for many more Leyland Nationals, most of which were sold to West Midlands Travel, where they were stored as a reserve fleet for some time, only a small number being actually prepared for service.

A Plaxton Pointer-bodied Dennis Dart demonstrator had been tried in the spring of 1995, and immediately following the second delivery of Lances 13 Darts arrived, mainly for rural services into Shropshire. These were to the standard specification of the Badgerline group, although this latter had by now (on 16 June) merged with Grampian to form FirstBus.

In the summer of 1996 there arrived a further Plaxton Pointer-bodied Dennis Dart, the company's first low-floor vehicle; this was intended for a series of Shropshire County Council contracts but later migrated to other Kidderminster duties. It introduced a new livery with more cream and the revised FirstBus-style **'Midland Red West'** fleetname accompanied by the group's '*f*' symbol. This fleetname was applied to other vehicles as they were repainted but was superseded from early 1998 by the group's new corporate style, whereby **'First'** was prominent, the local name being secondary. The latter was now just 'Midland Red', 'West' being dropped from both this and the company title, which became First Midland Red Buses Ltd.

At the end of 1996 a further Lance arrived on long-term loan from Plaxton, operating for some time

Above: The solitary low-floor Dennis Dart acquired in 1996 for Shropshire County Council tendered services later migrated to other Kidderminster routes, including the X33 hospital link, which had been inaugurated with second-hand minibuses. By the time it was photographed in Bromsgrove in March 2001 it had gained First fleetnames on its original cream-and-red livery.

in white before just the front panels were painted in red and cream. The following year was very quiet on the vehicle front, although the vehicle which joined the fleet in time for the new school year introduced a new combination, being a Mercedes-Benz 811D with Optare StarRider bodywork. It came from Western National and was repainted in standard livery.

Early in 1998 13 Lances left the fleet for other parts of the FirstBus empire, some to return in 'Barbie 2' days. Later in the year a large number of Mercedes-Benz L608Ds arrived from Brewers, although most were cannibalised for spares. Five entered service, not necessarily fully repainted, and their stay in the fleet was not long. The final second-hand addition of 1998 was a Plaxton Paramount 3200-bodied Leyland Tiger from the First Calderline unit of Yorkshire Rider.

The Mercedes-Benz minibuses for the Worcester operation had proved extremely robust, confounding their critics who had predicted short lives. Many of the original vehicles were still in use after nearly 13 years when replacement came on 1 August 1998 in the shape of 64 Plaxton Beaver 2 bodied Mercedes-Benz Varios, these taking to the road in the mainly cream livery introduced with the low-floor Dart two years earlier. These vehicles had standard FirstBus interiors but did not qualify for the original 'Barbie' livery because of their step entrances. In retrospect the replacement timing was unfortunate, and the Varios were to have relatively short lives in Worcester, being displaced by low-floor vehicles and dispersed to other First subsidiaries within five years.

Various low-floor demonstrators were tried in 1999, but none was added to the fleet, which soon became the last within FirstGroup without a 'Barbie'-liveried vehicle. Given that the operational fleet of Leyland Nationals had been reduced to around five vehicles, the only vehicles to join the fleet in 1999 came as something of a surprise, being two National 2s from Badgerline, only one of which gained fleet livery. Both outlasted the remaining Mk 1 Nationals, which were initially withdrawn early in 2001, although some were reinstated for another year.

In 2000 came yet more second-hand vehicles, all of which were given standard red-and-cream livery. Three Leyland Lynxes, almost identical to the indigenous vehicles except for matrix route-number displays, arrived from the Bristol Citybus fleet. They joined the main batch of Lynxes at Redditch and were later selected for 'Circle Line' route branding for the town's principal route. Altogether eight Lynxes were so branded, the most recent repaints being chosen.

The minibus fleet, much of which was now between 13 and 15 years old, was rejuvenated with the addition of nine Plaxton Beaver-bodied Mercedes-Benz 709Ds

Left: Purchased in 1998 for Worcester city services, the 64 Mercedes-Benz Vario minibuses with Plaxton Beaver 2 bodywork were soon rendered obsolete by the move to low-floor buses. This May 1999 view shows one leaving Bromsgrove on the rural service to Droitwich Spa.

Right: Five Dennis Dart SLFs with 34-seat Caetano Nimbus bodies joined the fleet in 2001 for operation on Worcester's first permanent park-and-ride service. They would receive corporate colours in 2008, when the company lost the contract.

from First Bradford and the first of 26 Frank Guy-converted 609Ds from Eastern Counties. Delivery of the latter extended into 2001, and the later arrivals became the fleet's first 'Barbie'-liveried vehicles, receiving the revised 'Barbie 2' style.

Until the Midland Red name was dropped the fleet continued to be free of the original 'Barbie' livery, despite the arrival of two batches of low-floor Dennis Darts. In the summer of 2000 two Plaxton Mini Pointer Darts, in white with red route branding, arrived for a new service linking Kidderminster and Worcester hospitals, introduced in the wake of NHS changes in Worcestershire. (The Kidderminster–Redditch hospital service, launched at the same time, had to make do with the ex-Bradford Beavers.) The MPDs were followed early in 2001 by five Caetano Nimbus-bodied Dart SLFs for Worcester's first permanent park-and-ride scheme. Although a Nimbus had appeared in First corporate colours at the previous year's NEC show,

the new buses were stock vehicles with a standard interior finish and a striking blue-and-orange external colour scheme.

In terms of the image presented to the public, the 'Midland Red' era was now over. A rebranding of First's bus activities would see the former Midland Red (West) operation described henceforth as 'First Wyvern', while in 2008 the company's legal name would be changed again, to 'First Midlands West Ltd'. No further vehicles were painted in the red-and-cream livery, although this was to survive on unrepainted vehicles for several years, some Dennis Lances still being red as late as 2006.

The heritage of Midland Red was, however, not lost on First Wyvern. In addition to restoring Midland Red's first Leyland National to its original, darker shade of red, it had one of the company's 2004/5 intake of Alexander Dennis Enviro300 low-floor single-deckers delivered in a commemorative red livery, which it was to carry for nearly three years.

Left: The Beaver 2s were among early repaints in corporate First colours, as shown by this well-loaded example heading to Kidderminster on the X33 from Redditch.

Right: The Plaxton Verde-bodied Dennis Lances also succumbed to First livery. This was one of the initial delivery of 37, which arrived in the spring of 1994.

'Sixties Yorkshire

Geoff Mills looks at Yorkshire's municipal bus fleets in the 1960s and finds plenty of variety.

Left: Doncaster Corporation standardised on Roe bodywork, as seen on this 1963 Daimler CVG6-30 at work in 1964. The open door clearly shows the three-step entrance, a layout considered perfectly acceptable at that time. Note also the simple bus-stop sign. This bus seated 72, which was a typical figure for a 30ft-long forward-entrance double-decker.

Right: Doncaster operated trolleybuses until 1963. This 1946 Sunbeam W was acquired from Southend Corporation in 1954, at which time it had a 56-seat Park Royal body. Doncaster fitted a new 62-seat Roe body in 1957 and when the Karrier was withdrawn in 1962 transferred the five-year-old body to a motor-bus chassis. Doncaster's livery at this time was a dark red.

Top: Roe-bodied Daimlers featured prominently in the Rotherham Corporation fleet in the 1960s and included six 78-seat Fleetlines delivered in 1968.

Above: In the early-postwar years Rotherham bought Bristols, both double-deck Ks and single-deck Ls. This 1950 L5G has a 32-seat East Lancs body. The centre-entrance layout was favoured by a small number of urban operators.

Left: Sheffield's Joint Omnibus Committee — part-owned by British Railways — gave the fleet access to ECW bodies which, in the 1950s and early 1960s, could be supplied only to state-owned operators. This saw Sheffield receive ECW bodies on Leyland chassis, both Titan double-deckers and Leopard single-deckers. This 1961 Leopard has a 41-seat body of a style usually seen on Bristol MW chassis.

Right: Alexander bodywork was quite rare in England until the early 1960s and the success of its stylish body for Atlantean and Fleetline chassis. In 1960 Sheffield took twenty 69-seat Alexander bodies on 30ft-long AEC Regent V chassis. Rear-entrance 30ft Alexander bodies were rare, the only other big user being Cardiff City Transport, on Guy Arab chassis.

Left: This attractive style of East Lancs body was specified by a few English municipal fleets, including Sheffield, operator of this 1964 Leyland Atlantean. It was a PDR1/2 chassis with a drop-centre rear axle, which eliminated the step in the gangway. The body on this bus was actually built in Sheffield at East Lancs' associated Neepsend factory.

Right: The Halifax fleet was both colourful — its livery was orange, green and cream — and varied. This Daimler CVG6 with 61-seat Roe body was one of 12 delivered in 1954. It is seen in the town 10 years later.

Below: Later Halifax buses featured forward entrances, as on this 1966 Leyland Titan PD2/37 with 64-seat Weymann body, photographed in 1967.

Top: A gleaming East Lancs-bodied Daimler CVG6-30 in the Huddersfield Corporation fleet in 1967. The dark translucent panel behind the driver's cab was designed to add extra illumination to the staircase. This bus was part of the Corporation's trolleybus-replacement fleet. The last Huddersfield trolleybus ran in 1968.

Above: Huddersfield — like Halifax, Todmorden and Sheffield — had a Joint Omnibus Committee which combined the interests of the Corporation and British Railways. This JOC-owned bus, a Guy Arab UF with 43-seat Guy body, does not carry the town's coat of arms. New in 1952, it is seen here in 1967.

Right: Leeds City Transport was West Yorkshire's biggest municipal bus operator. Its early-postwar intake of new buses included 20 Crossley DD42/7 models, delivered in 1959. Crossley built the 56-seat body. This is a 1963 view.

Left: Most Leeds buses were bodied locally by Roe, whose factory was at Crossgates, in the east of the city. However, bodies were also purchased from other suppliers, including Metro-Cammell, which supplied Orion bodies on AEC, Daimler and Leyland chassis. This is a 1955 Titan PD2/11. The window by the staircase at the rear of the lower deck was a common feature on Roe bodies but was unusual on an Orion.

Right: A 1957 Daimler CVG6 with 60-seat Orion body waits in city centre traffic in 1967. When it switched to rear-engined models Leeds continued to divide its orders between Britain's three leading chassis manufacturers, taking Swifts from AEC, Fleetlines from Daimler and Atlanteans from Leyland.

Top: The purchase of second-hand buses by municipal operators was rare in the 1950s, but a few took advantage of the premature withdrawal by London Transport of some of its AEC Regents. This RT-class Regent III was 11 years old when it joined the Bradford Corporation fleet in 1958. It had a Park Royal body.

Above: Bradford was Britain's last trolleybus operator, the system closing in 1972. It operated a mixed fleet, and this modern-looking BUT is not quite what it seems. The 66-seat East Lancs body was new in 1962, but the chassis had been new to Darlington Corporation in 1949. It then passed to Doncaster in 1952 and to Bradford in 1959.

Where are they now?

All of Yorkshire's former municipal bus operations are now run by First. Those in West Yorkshire became part of the new West Yorkshire PTE in 1974. Its bus operations were taken over by the PTE-owned Yorkshire Rider business in 1986, which was privatised in an employee buy-out two years later. It was then purchased by Badgerline in 1994. Badgerline merged with GRT in 1995 to create FirstBus. First operates some 1,150 buses in its West Yorkshire fleets.

The story in South Yorkshire is similar, with the South Yorkshire PTE taking over in 1974, a new PTE-owned South Yorkshire Transport becoming the bus operator in 1986, and a buy-out following in 1993. The SYT business was bought by First in 1998. Today First's South Yorkshire fleet numbers 580 buses.

Below: Yorkshire's urban buses are run today by First. These include Wright StreetCars on the 'ftr' service in Leeds. Stewart J. Brown

The quest for capacity

Over the years a recurring theme in bus design is the desire to maximise capacity. **Stewart J. Brown** considers why operators are usually — though not always — looking for bigger buses.

Look back over the history of British bus building and you'll find a recurrent theme: the search for increased carrying capacity. For example, 50 years ago there was a major increase in double-deck carrying capacity as new length regulations were enacted at the same time as Leyland was developing its rear-engined Atlantean chassis. Typical seating capacity rose from around 60 in a nominal 27ft 6in-long front-engined bus to around 70 in a 30-footer, and to a maximum of 78 — that's an increase of 30% — in the new generation of rear-engined buses. For single-deckers, capacity rose from 45 to 53 — almost 20% — when the length regulations were relaxed in 1961, from a maximum of 30ft to 36ft.

By increasing capacity operators were — in theory, at least — able to carry the same number of people

MORE SEATS

GREATER COMFORT

EASIER ACCESS

MORE ECONOMICAL OPERATING

Left: Among the selling-points highlighted by Alexander on this Atlantean brochure 50 years ago was a simple message: More seats. The drawing is based on the first body built by Alexander on an Atlantean, a bus for Glasgow Corporation, whose purchases in the 1960s would in the main be 78-seat Atlanteans.

Above right: But even conventional half-cab 30-footers offered high capacity. This AEC/Park Royal Bridgemaster for Southend Corporation seated 76. It was new in 1959. *Harry Hay*

in fewer vehicles. The downside of that was that service frequencies could then be reduced. Three 78-seaters running every 20 minutes provided almost as much capacity as four 60-seaters running every 15 minutes. So operators saved money, but passengers got an inferior service. However, if you factor in the extra costs of running complex rear-engined models with inferior fuel efficiency and poorer reliability, it may be that the savings were more imagined than real. The mid-1960s saw a new interest in 'standee' single-deckers. These had lower seating capacity —

say 46 in a typical two-door rear-engined model, down from 53 in a single-door mid-engined bus — but this was balanced by increased standing capacity and the opportunity to dispense with the services of a conductor, substantially reducing the operator's wage bill.

It was a nice idea, but not a successful one. In the 1960s most bus passengers felt hard done by if they didn't get a seat in return for their 6d fare, and standee buses were universally unpopular. So cities which tried them in significant numbers — Leeds, Liverpool,

Right: The Alexander W type was fitted to low-frame rear-engined chassis — the AEC Swift, Leyland Panther and, as seen here, the Daimler Fleetline. The biggest user of W-type bodies on Fleetlines was the Northern General group, which took 41 in 1971. They were dual-door 40-seaters. This example is seen in Sunderland. *Stewart J. Brown*

London — were soon returning to double-deckers in the 1970s. In some cases these were 33ft-long models, which allowed the use of two doors while retaining the carrying capacity of a single-door 30ft bus.

The pursuit of capacity saw Daimler produce a 36ft-long double-decker for Walsall in 1968, with a dual-door 86-seat Northern Counties body. Based on a CRC6-36 chassis, it remained unique in Britain, although similar chassis were exported to South Africa.

In the 1970s the quest for maximum capacity was no longer the only aim of urban operators. Many opted to specify fewer seats than the 78 which had in effect been the standard figure in the 1960s, instead going for 74 or 75. Others — Nottingham being the prime

example — still sought to maximise the number of seats. In Nottingham's case a clever internal layout and the use of a narrow entrance door saw up to 80 seats being fitted to a 9.5m-long Atlantean with two doors — a quite remarkable achievement.

Then, in the 1980s, the world was turned upside down. Suddenly 16-seaters were all the rage. The 1960s aim of fewer, bigger buses was abandoned. Now operators were focused on service frequency. To provide the same capacity as two 48-seat Leyland Nationals running every 30 minutes required six Ford Transits operating every 10 minutes. Setting aside for a moment the relative merits of a soundly engineered, purpose-built, heavy-duty bus against a lightweight

Left: Dual-door buses were for a short time viewed as essential if they were to be one-man-operated. An early user of this layout was Newcastle Corporation, as apparent from this Alexander-bodied Atlantean in the demonstration park at the 1968 Commercial Motor Show in London. Uniquely, Newcastle specified a nearside staircase, hence the blank panel ahead of the exit door. This bus seated 70, at a time when a single-door Atlantean normally had 78 seats. *Harry Hay*

Right: The rear-engined double-decker with one door and around 76 seats — typified by this Blackburn Corporation Atlantean — became the urban standard. This bus was bodied locally by East Lancs, for many years the main supplier of the town's bus bodies. *Stewart J. Brown*

Right: In 1986
deregulation turned
the industry on its head.
Out went the quest for
capacity, and in came the
need for higher service
frequencies. This was
achieved with small buses,
initially 16-seaters —
but soon growing to
buses with 20 or 25 seats.
In 1987 newly independent
PMT took 25 Dodge S56s
with 20-seat Alexander
bodies. *Stewart J. Brown*

van-based minibus, try asking yourself how long, having just missed your local bus, you would prefer to wait for the next one — 9 minutes or 29 minutes?

But here again the quest for increased capacity quickly reappeared. Operators were soon looking for buses with more than 16 seats, and very soon 20-seaters were being specified, based on heavier vehicles than the Transit and its competitors. In some cases this was to increase capacity. One-for-one replacement of 16-seaters with 20-seaters gave a straightforward 25% increase in seats. But in others it was the 1960s cycle of service reduction all over again. If you had a fleet of five minibuses with 16 seats running on a service every 12 minutes, you could provide the same capacity with four 20-seaters every 15 minutes.

And so small buses grew ever bigger. The Transits were succeeded by van-based Mercedes-Benz L608Ds, which in turn were replaced by 25-seat coach-built models based on the 609D and 709D chassis and the Iveco Daily — and by the stylish VW-based Optare CityPacer. Heavier chassis from Mercedes and from Renault saw small buses growing to 33 seats. You don't have to be a mathematician to work out that one 33-seat Mercedes could replace two 16-seat Transits.

Then came the Dennis Dart. This bus more than any other defined the British bus industry in the late 1980s and much of the 1990s. The Dart was originally a 28-seater, 8.5m long, designed to offer big-bus convenience on routes operated by small buses.

Front-engined truck-based small buses had a lot going for them. They were cheap to buy. Spares were cheap — a replacement engine for a 609D cost about the same as a replacement gearbox for a double-

decker. Drivers were, generally, paid less than those at the wheel of a 'proper' bus. But these vehicles were noisy. The ride quality was poor. And while small buses lasted in service for much longer than anyone had expected, they did require more maintenance.

So the Dart was offered as an alternative. It was like a scaled-down big bus, purpose-designed for bus operation. And it grew. The original 8.5m model quickly proved to be something of a minority interest. Most were operated in London. So there was soon a 9m version, and then a 9.8m.

The move to low-floor buses in the mid-1990s hit carrying capacity. A side-effect of lowering the floor was to increase wheel-arch intrusion and thus reduce floor space, and the need to provide space for wheelchairs and 'baby buggies' further compromised seating capacity. To maintain carrying capacity the low-floor version of the Dart had to be longer than its predecessor. Indeed the Dart SLF — Super Low Floor — would ultimately be stretched to create the 11.3m Super Dart. And remember this was a model which had been designed to compete with the Mercedes 709D and was still viewed by some as a midibus. The Super Dart was the same size as a Leyland National.

The move to low-floor vehicles saw a growing number of operators of single-deck buses make full use of the maximum 12m length. Although 12m single-deck buses were legal from as early as 1969, most operators were content to use vehicles of around 11m in length. Leyland's National stretched this to 11.3m — and then to 11.6m with the National 2 — but it was really only with the arrival of full-size low-floor buses that 12m became the standard length for an urban single-decker. When it launched the Enviro300 in 2001,

TransBus stretched the model to an optional 12.5m length to increase seating capacity to a headline-grabbing maximum of 45. It seems churlish to point out that this was the same as a 30ft-long (9.1m) single-decker in the 1960s.

Meanwhile double-deck sales were in the doldrums. A typical 1980s 9.5m double-decker seated around 75, and that remained the same into the 1990s. In 1989 Stagecoach, which was then buying long-wheelbase Leyland Olympians with 87-seat low-height Alexander bodies, took delivery of three 11m-long three-axle examples, again bodied by Alexander: two seated 96, the third having a UK record of 110 seats. Clearly the benefits of the extra length and increased capacity were not enough to convince Stagecoach that three-axle buses were the answer.

As on single-deckers, the introduction of low-floor double-deckers cut capacity. Most early examples were dual-door models for London operators. In a

9.5m-long Volvo Olympian the typical seating capacity on a dual-door London bus was 72; that figure dropped to as low as 62 on early 10.6m-long DAFs. Compare that with 64 in a 27ft 6in (8.4m) Routemaster of 40 years earlier — and which was also about three tons lighter — and you could be forgiven for asking about the price of progress.

So, once again, buses got bigger, many operators of double-deckers specifying vehicles of around 11m in length, and some — Lothian Buses, for example — even managing just over 11m on two-axle Volvo B7TLs with Wright bodies.

Adding a third axle increases gross vehicle weight from 18 tonnes to 24.5 tonnes, and this in turn increases carrying capacity. There are a small number of three-axle double-deckers in regular UK service, most being buses imported from Africa or Hong Kong by Stagecoach. In Ireland, Dublin Bus runs a batch of three-axle Volvo B9TLs with 91-seat Alexander Dennis

Right: Early low-floor single-deckers seated fewer people than the previous generation of step-entrance models. A typical Dennis Lance, for example, seated 49, whereas this low-floor Lance SLF had just 40 seats, a reduction of almost 20%. Wright was one of the pioneers of accessible buses in the UK and bodied this Lance SLF operated by London & Country. New in 1995, it is seen in Croydon.
Stewart J. Brown

Left: A 1996 Volvo Olympian in the fleet of Bullock of Cheadle illustrates the soon-to-be-obsolete step-entrance double-decker. It had a 77-seat Northern Counties body. Behind is a 1991 Dennis Dominator in the Stagecoach Magicbus fleet, also with a Northern Counties body; it seated 72.
Stewart J. Brown

Enviro500 bodies. First Glasgow has ten 12m-long three-axle B9TLs with bodywork by East Lancs. They seat 95.

Using two decks to carry more people is not a uniquely British concept, but British operators and manufacturers have long been the main proponents of the idea. Hong Kong is a major user of British-style double-deckers, while Germany has its own particular version, just 4m high, which has a long history.

But in continental Europe the quest for added capacity has generally been met by using articulated buses rather than double-deckers. There was brief interest in artics in Britain in the late 1970s and early 1980s, which saw left-hand-drive demonstrators from Volvo, Leyland DAB and Mercedes-Benz being inspected by operators. South Yorkshire PTE purchased artics, many of which later saw service elsewhere — from Bath to Barrhead — but that was about it.

Fast forward almost 20 years, and London is looking at increasing capacity on its transport system. The answer is more buses. And bigger buses. Enter the artic. The first were introduced to Red Arrow services in 2002. Then more appeared on trunk routes on some of the capital's busiest corridors. Today there are mote than 400 artics in operation in London, all of them Mercedes-Benz Citaros. Maximum seating capacity is not the aim — with 49 seats they carry fewer seated passengers than a Routemaster — but total capacity is 135. That compares with a maximum of 91 (with 67 seated) in a London-specification Enviro400.

Factors which mitigate against artics include their size. They are 18m long, so need more depot space than a double-decker. But, going back to some simple arithmetic, if an artic can carry 135 people while a double-decker carries only 91, then for every three double-deckers you need only two artics. So the depot space required to provide the same service capacity

Above: The latest generation of low-floor double-deckers is typified by a Volvo B7TL in the First Leeds fleet. It has a 74-seat Wright body. *Stewart J. Brown*

Above right: Three-axle double-deckers offer increased carrying capacity, but few have been bought new by British operators. Most of those that are in regular UK service are ex-Hong Kong vehicles, such as this Magicbus Leyland Olympian in Manchester. *Stewart J. Brown*

using artics is greater, by about 25%. Artics also require more workshop space and are trickier to manoeuvre, particularly in reverse. But, contrary to popular belief, they are just as manoeuvrable in traffic as any other type of bus, although they do, of course, take up more space on the road, as well as at bus stops and in bus stations.

Outside London artics are few and far between. First runs Volvo-based Wright Streetcars in York and Leeds and will soon be introducing them to Swansea. These carry up to 127 people, with 37 seated. First also runs conventional Volvo and Scania artics in Glasgow and Manchester, among other places. Elsewhere articulated buses tend to be used on specialised services such as Truronian's Citaros at The Eden Project or Go North East's Scanias on a shuttle service in Gateshead.

A new approach to high-capacity single-deckers was tried by Stagecoach in 2007 with the introduction of three-axle Scanias to services in Fife. These were 13.7m-long low-entry OmniLink models, with 56 high-backed seats. Setting aside odd vehicles like the electric Tecnobus midibuses operated by Selwyns

Left: Dublin Bus operates three-axle Volvo B9TLs with Alexander Dennis Enviro500 bodywork. They are 91-seaters. *Stewart J. Brown*

in St Helens, these, along with broadly similar vehicles for Nottingham, were the first new three-axle single-deck buses for a British operator since the Bedford VAL of four decades earlier.

Much has changed in the British bus industry in the 50 years since operators saw 30ft-long double-deckers as a way of increasing capacity and cutting costs. Foremost among these changes has been a drop in the number of people travelling by bus, from 13,000,000,000 a year to 4,500,000,000.

So, in 2008, while there are still many areas where capacity is an issue, there is also a much stronger focus on passenger comfort and on tailoring capacity to the requirements of different types of route. It is an over-simplification, but turn the clock back 25 years and operators were buying just two types of bus: a 74-seat double-decker or a 51-seat single-decker. There was little else available.

Now there is a huge range of sizes. The Alexander Dennis range alone embraces Enviro200 and 300 models with standard seating capacities from 26 to 49 (or even 60, with three-plus-two seating). For smaller buses Optare has Solos offering from 23 to 37 seats — this being another example of a model which started out small and gradually grew bigger — and if you need more capacity then there are artics from Mercedes-Benz, Scania and Wrightbus.

Of course, if you really need high carrying capacity there's always the bi-articulated bus, carrying up to 300 people ...

Left: The bus which led the market right through the 1990s was the Dennis Dart, and this has been reinvented by Alexander Dennis as the Enviro200 Dart, still offering a range of seating capacities. This is the smallest model, a 29-seater with a nominal length of 9m, in the fleet of West Coast Motor Services. New in 2007, it is based in Dunoon. The biggest Enviro200 Dart is 11.3m long and seats 40. *Stewart J. Brown*

Trolleybus encounters

Michael H. C. Baker recalls the trolleybus systems he has come across, from Bournemouth in the 1940s to present-day San Francisco.

All photographs by the author or from the author's collection

Although London Transport had the biggest trolleybus fleet in the world, and one of its routes was a few minutes' walk from where I was brought up in Thornton Heath, it was the highly distinctive yellow trolleybuses of Bournemouth which as a young lad I knew best and upon which I travelled each day to and from school.

Bombed out of our house in the summer of 1944, we fled to the seaside in Hampshire (as it then was), where Dad's office had transferred him to a requisitioned hotel on the cliff tops and we found accommodation over a grocer's in the town centre.

Bournemouth grew up around a series of valleys, or chines, leading back from the sea, and the principal gathering-point for public transport, then as now, was The Square — which isn't square at all. Underneath it passes the stream, 'river' being too grand a word for this trickle of water, the Bourne, from which the town derives its name.

Bournemouth is a recent town by English standards, its population in 1861 being but 1,707 whilst by 1900, after the coming of the railway, it had reached 67,771. But it has always considered itself both modern and socially quite definitely superior. Thus by the 1930s it determined to rid itself of its old-fashioned trams and invest in a fleet of modern, elegant and almost silent trolleybuses. Most municipalities might have chosen a livery where either red or green predominated, but Bournemouth's yellow was both distinctive and somewhat exclusive.

After experimenting with several makes it settled on Sunbeam as a chassis supplier — yellow Sunbeams being a nice coincidence — with bodies by Park Royal and English Electric. The latter faithfully copied the former. Officially the livery was 'primrose', with two maroon bands, olive-green and red lining, the town's coat of arms and off-white roofs, although by 1944 the roofs were maroon. It looked splendid. Bournemouth loved its trolleybuses, which seemed to blend in so well with its image of sedate refinement, and kept them, right to the end, in excellent condition.

Our local route was the 25A, which ran from Ashley Road, Boscombe, to Westbourne. We used it both when arriving by train from Waterloo at the Central station and on school journeys to Westbourne Preparatory School. Westbourne was served by a loop, and on alighting there I would proceed through the front door of my school, which was in Hampshire; had I used the back I would have found myself in Dorset. The school's address was County Gates, and although Bournemouth has long ago been moved into Dorset — not without protest — older residents still refer to the area as such. Most surprisingly a box containing electrical apparatus and adorned with the Bournemouth coat of arms is still on the pavement there.

The trams which the trolleybuses replaced in 1935/6 had crossed the border into Poole, but the council there decided that Hants & Dorset motor buses would take the place of trams. Thus when we visited my grandmother in Poole High Street each Wednesday we would travel in a Hants & Dorset Titan.

At the beginning of the war, with no holidaymakers, a number of Bournemouth trolleybuses were loaned elsewhere, including some which came to London to work in the Barking area, although as far as I was concerned this was as distant from Thornton Heath as Vladivostok, and I certainly never got to see them. By 1944/5 Bournemouth was awash with American soldiers, on their way to fight across the Channel, and in my experience the trolleys were always packed.

Bournemouth trolleybuses had two staircases and a front exit, but unless my memory is totally at fault I have no recollection of ever using the front one, any more than I alighted from the front exit of the 'Feltham' tram which completed the final part of our journey home from Waterloo in June 1945 — too late for the VE Day street party but in plenty of time for the VJ Day one.

When the time came to abandon trams, not all South Coast towns switched to trolleybuses, but three did — Portsmouth, Brighton and Hastings. None of these fleets could match Bournemouth in size or, indeed, in longevity, although Hastings took to trolleybuses rather earlier. Known as the Hastings Tramways Co, it was bought by Maidstone & District

Right: A 1935
Bournemouth Sunbeam S2
with two-door 56-seat
Park Royal body. This bus
was withdrawn in 1952,
but others from the same
batch served the town
for 25 years.

Left: Bournemouth's
last trolleybuses were
Sunbeams with stylish
Weymann bodies,
delivered in 1962.
This is a similar bus
from an earlier delivery
— in 1959 — approaching
The Square.

in 1935, and its vehicles were painted in that
company's dignified livery of deep green and off-white,
boldly emblazoned, even in postwar years, with
'HASTINGS TRAMWAYS'. Many of its trolleys had Weymann
bodies, rather like those in Brighton.

On a visit to St Leonards on a quiet, rather grey
Sunday in October 1954 I managed to insinuate myself
into the company's Silverhill depot. There I found much
of the fleet enjoying its day of rest. There were the
expected late-prewar and early-postwar Weymann-
and Park Royal-bodied Sunbeams and AECs, plus the
already quite famous open-topper, a 1928 Dodson-
bodied Guy. Relegated to the service fleet at the
beginning of World War 2, this had been restored to

passenger service and suitably decorated for the
Queen's coronation in 1953, after which it appeared
quite regularly in the summer months.

The open-topper is still with us. After the last
Hastings trolleybuses ceased service in June 1959
it was fitted with a Commer diesel engine and, known
as 'Happy Harold' on account of having conveyed
Harold of Wessex to his fateful meeting with William
of Normandy back in 1066 (or maybe it just looked
as if it was old enough to have done so), it has
become a regular on the rally circuit.

There can be few greater contrasts in English towns
than that between Bournemouth and Huddersfield,
but some 20 years after the end of the war I travelled

regularly across the Pennines and through the Yorkshire mill town and discovered that it too owned a fleet of six-wheel double-deck trolleybuses. I was living in Liverpool and Southport at the time and used regularly to visit friends in Leeds. This was long before the M62 was built, and I would take the A62 from Oldham up over the edge of Saddleworth Moor and so to Huddersfield. More often than not I would find myself and my trusty Citroën Light 15 following a big, red, stately Roe- or East Lancs-bodied six-wheeler through the town's main streets and out on the Leeds Road. Our first meeting would be at Marsden, the best part of six miles from the town centre and amid typical Pennine — *i.e.* stunningly beautiful — scenery.

Bournemouth may have considered itself posh, but visually Huddersfield and its surroundings knocked it into a cocked hat, the grandeur of the moors, valleys and mills being quite incomparable. I'm well aware that smoking mill chimneys probably have a romantic appeal only to a southerner, especially an art student with a liking for L. S. Lowry, and I was only too conscious of the fact that many of my colleagues at Southport and Liverpool art colleges came from families where generations had worked in cotton mills, coal mines, glass works and so forth and found absolutely nothing to recommend such occupations. But in its own way the Huddersfield area was (and, indeed, is) a visual delight, and the town's big, handsome, well-cared-for trolleybuses contributed to its unique character.

Huddersfield had actually been the very first British local authority to operate public transport, back in 1883. At that time it ran trams, and when they began to fall out of favour at the beginning of the 1930s it turned to the trolleybus. By 1940, when the system was complete, it was extensive and complex, serving some 16 destinations to all points of the compass out into the Pennines.

Above: The conductor of this Portsmouth AEC trolleybus is removing the pole which was stowed beneath the vehicle to rescue the collector booms, which have de-wired. Note the ornate lining on the corner panels, the comprehensive destination display and the 'STOP'/ trafficator sign under the lower-deck window. Hovis is still with us; Timothy Whites was taken over by Boots in the 1960s, although the name survived until the 1980s.

Right: Huddersfield offered dramatic backdrops for its trolleybuses, with its hilly terrain.

Left: The chassis of this Huddersfield trolleybus dates from 1938, but the 66-seat Roe body was built in 1951 as part of a programme of upgrading the fleet.
D. A. Jones

One hazard of operating in such hilly territory was the possibility of falling off a Pennine. I jest not, for that is exactly what befell one of the final BUT vehicles. No suitable spot for a reversing triangle or circle could be found at Longwood, terminus of a route to the south-west of the town, so the trolleybuses had to reverse out onto a circle built over a valley. One day in February 1967 — yes, it was the 13th, since you ask — something went horribly wrong, and a trolleybus fell into the field below, thankfully without fatal consequences.

Karrier was the favoured supplier in prewar days, whilst Sunbeam and BUT built many of the postwar vehicles. The very last six-wheel trolleybuses built for use in England were 10 Sunbeams with East Lancs bodies supplied to Huddersfield in 1958/9 — very nice,

and the epitome of Huddersfield trolleybuses as I remember them. Many of the prewar vehicles, as well as some of the early-postwar examples, were rebodied by Roe and East Lancs, and these dominated the fleet in its final years. In 1962, following the national trend, the local authority decided that the days of the trolleybus were numbered. And so vehicles that had for more than 30 years been the pride of Huddersfield made their final journeys on 13 July 1968.

Well, not quite — for one of the four preserved vehicles, a 1959 Sunbeam, was taken south a year later to Reading, which was one of six towns still operating trolleybuses. Following an extensive tour there it decided, having got this far south, to go the whole hog and visit the seaside at — yes, wait for it — Bournemouth, one of the other five towns still with trolleybuses. There, one Sunday in November ('in brilliant sunshine', to quote the West Yorkshire Transport Circle's 1983 *Huddersfield Trolleybus Memories*), it completed an 85-mile tour, Bournemouth Transport Department charging the owners £2 6s 1d for electricity (which was considered 'very reasonable'). The cost of towing the bus all the way from Yorkshire to Bournemouth and back was something over £60.

Today the Sunbeam is still at work, albeit in semi-retirement, in Yorkshire, in the care of the British Trolleybus Society at Sandtoft.

The direct route from Huddersfield to Leeds was through Mirfield and Liversedge, but I would frequently find myself in Bradford. This, perhaps, is set even more spectacularly amongst the Pennines than is Huddersfield. Although it got rather messed around in the 1960s, and some fairly horrible buildings went up, it has kept some of its fine 19th-century architecture, not least its city hall, which, along with that in Manchester, is among the finest in the land. At this point I will now introduce my mother-in-law. Well, somewhat obliquely, which is probably the best way.

As is well known, Bradford had the distinction of operating trolleybuses after every other British town and city had abandoned them. In 1970, recently married, my wife and I had invited my parents-in-law over from Ireland for a holiday Up North, not least because my wife, Maeve, had been taught by the nuns in her convent school in a remote part of Connemara, all about the cotton towns of Yorkshire — in Irish,

I might add. This had proved immensely useful when she went on to study maths at university in Dublin, and she was determined to find out if Dewsbury, Wakefield, Bradford etc were all that the nuns had led her to believe. I, on the other hand, had taken Maeve up to Belfast the year before we were married to ride on a trolleybus there and discovered that, whilst not much thrilled by this, she had at least not broken our engagement. So I submitted all three relations to a trip out to Duckworth Lane, where they patiently waited whilst I photographed the last remnants of what had once been a feature of so many British towns and cities. (Here I must pay tribute to both parents-in-law, who over the years have sat in a number of less-than-inviting locations, without complaint, whilst I have photographed all manner of vehicles.) I cannot say whether they noticed just how unusual was Bradford's fleet by this time, for many of the vehicles, like contemporary double-deck motor buses, had forward entrances. At its peak the fleet numbered around 200, and, as other trolleybus fleets faded away in the 1950s and 1960s, so Bradford bought examples from them and had them rebodied.

Bradford could lay claim to be the home of the British trolleybus, for although it couldn't compare in size with London it operated trolleybuses far longer. They started in 1911, and by the time the last one ran into Thornbury depot on 26 March 1972 electric traction — tram and trolley — had graced the city's streets for more than 70 years.

Left: Bradford's Duckworth Lane depot in September 1970, some 18 months before the end of trolleybus operation. Forward-entrance trolleybuses were relatively rare. The vehicles seen here started life as single-deckers with the Mexborough & Swinton Traction Co and were rebodied by East Lancs for operation in Bradford.

Right: A reminder of Belfast's trolleybus fleet is provided by this 1948 Harkness-bodied Guy BTX on display at the Ulster Folk & Transport Museum.

Belfast was mentioned in passing, so we'll now head across the Irish Sea whilst noting that this was the only place in all the 32 counties which operated trolleybuses. I have to record that on my first visit in 1961 there was much which reminded me of a northern English city, not least its trolleybuses. Although most of them were bodied locally, by Harkness, their chassis came from England, and the big six-wheelers, in their livery of deep red and off-white, were impressive and stately as all six-wheel trolleybuses tended to be and would not have looked out of place on many an English system. Their end came in May 1968.

Although the UK gave up trolleybus operation almost 40 years ago, this method of transport still has its advocates in mainland Europe, especially in Italy and Switzerland — each of which has 15 systems —

and beyond. The Italians are keen on both running and manufacturing trolleybuses, and last year I was in Rome and Naples, cities where they can be seen, admittedly not in very large numbers, trams being rather more popular.

Built by the same manufacturer as the Istanbul vehicles, Ansaldobreda of Bologna, but vastly more up-to-date, the Naples vehicles dated from 2000/1. They appeared to be operating just one route, from the central station, although a second is being added. Rome's sole trolleybus route is operated by even more-modern vehicles — Hungarian-built Solaris/Ganz artics delivered in 2005. The route was introduced on 23 March that year, 33 years after the last of the previous generation of Rome trolleybuses had quit the capital's streets. Naples calls its trolleys 'filobuses', Rome preferring *'trollini'*.

**Right:** Switzerland has 15 trolleybus networks. This is Zurich in 1993, with a 1960s FBW artic.

Above: The depot at Piraeus in 1993, with Italian-built trolleybuses ready for service.

Piraeus, the port for Athens and home probably to more passenger-carrying ships than any other in the world, ranging from ferries to cruise liners, introduced trolleybuses in 1949, five years before Athens itself. I was there some 15 years ago, and the trolleybuses were impossible to ignore, zooming up and down the hills, San Francisco-fashion, and beneath the Acropolis — just like Rome trams which skirt the now happily lion-free Colosseum. A route linking the Athens and Piraeus trolleybus systems was inaugurated in 1990, and now they are operated as one, all the vehicles I knew (which in Athens were Russian-built, in Piraeus Italian) having been replaced in time for the 2004 Olympics.

It is now time, clasping enough packs of sandwiches and thermos flasks of hot tea to prevent us from succumbing to caviar, kebab and vodka poisoning, to venture much further afield, namely to Moscow and St Petersburg by way of Istanbul. In all of these cities I encountered trolleybuses, yet in none could these be called stately, and in at least one a trolleybus ride provided an excellent opportunity to be robbed — which I, always ready to immerse myself in the local *ambience*, duly was.

I first visited Istanbul in 1966, and in those days on the European side of the Bosphorus Italian-built Ansaldo trolleybuses ran past our hotel and down to the waterfront, where the ferries linked Europe and Asia. Road surfaces left something to be desired, being a mixture of tarmac, cobbles and holes, and the trolleybuses bounced and shook as they rattled their

way up and down beneath the walls of Topkapi, the Sultans' palace, in this most cosmopolitan of cities.

I wouldn't say my experiences of trolleybuses in Russia have much to do with the future. In some ways it is a country still struggling to escape from its past, and this certainly includes just about every form of public transport. The only cities of which I have any first-hand knowledge are Moscow and St Petersburg, although when I first visited the latter it was known as Leningrad. That was back in 1967, and when I was there again — and in Moscow — some 35 years later not a lot seemed to have changed, in that the trams and trolleybuses looked old-fashioned and were badly maintained and overcrowded.

Of course, in other ways Russia — no longer the Soviet Union — had changed utterly. Which was quite obvious from the fashion sense of the young people, the music, the resurgence of church building and the middle-aged businessmen with their dark glasses in swanky restaurants, accompanied by young women at most half their age, with big, flashy Mercedes parked outside, blithely ignoring parking restrictions. The ordinary Russian had to make do with public transport. Whilst I was probably a tad unlucky, I managed to get robbed three times within a fortnight — once by a bus stop, once on a train and once on a trolleybus.

A ZiU in the Moscow fleet, pictured beneath the walls of the
Kremlin in 2001.

Above: St Petersburg was still known as Leningrad when this ZiU trolleybus was photographed in 1987. Vehicles of this type were still in service in the city at the start of the 21st century.

St Petersburg, like Moscow, has an extensive trolleybus network, as well as an equally extensive and very badly maintained tram system, and Maeve and I used both on a number of occasions. One morning we were heading for the Hermitage, the world-famous museum facing the city's wonderful waterfront. The trolley was jam-packed, and I had to hold on to the grab rail above my head with both hands. As we approached our stop I tried to extract myself from the crowd and suddenly felt my wallet being removed. I tried to turn around, and finding myself surrounded by several large men, shouted to my wife, who, already alighting, yelled: "Just get out!" Which I did.

Luckily I had very little money, but my cards were lost too. We managed to get these cancelled after hours spent in a police station; manned by perfectly obliging policemen (and women), this was in a tatty office block which looked as if it had been furnished by a very early Oxfam store, where ballpoint pens and even pencils were at a premium, telephones resembled those in a BT museum and computers belonged to a world beyond imagining.

Moscow and St Petersburg trolleybuses are not actually much older than those found in some Western European towns and cities, particularly Italy; they simply look archaic and are badly in need of tender loving care. The very first trolleybuses began work in Moscow in 1933, and 70 years later a parade was held to mark the event. I was not a little surprised to learn that some of the earliest were actually of British origin and, indeed, were double-deckers. Now I have never seen a double-deck trolleybus anywhere outside the UK, but English Electric supplied a fleet of just such to Moscow in 1935/6, to which were added others, the last being some BUT 9611Ts in 1948. All, of course, are long gone.

The state-run firm of ZiU had a virtual monopoly in postwar Soviet days and produced thousands of trolleybuses, many of which are still at work in Moscow, St Petersburg and all over Russia and beyond. There are around 50 routes in Moscow, and they are, as one guide put it, 'much favoured by pensioners, students and others with subsidised travel and consequently very crowded'. The situation is much the same in St Petersburg, although perhaps the trolleybuses are in slightly better nick than that city's trams, if only because they don't have to contend with the atrocious trackwork. However, many of the main streets are bedevilled with potholes, which go some way to evening the score. The tram system is the biggest in the world and in 2007 celebrated its centenary. The trolleybus came on the scene in 1936.

In 1990, the year the old Soviet Union disintegrated, the St Petersburg fleet numbered some 1,300 vehicles and carried some 550 million passengers. By 1999, with almost total reliance on public transport no longer the case, the trolleybus fleet had been reduced to around 900, of which some 30% were over 16 years old. In 1999 a detailed survey by a Swedish consultant suggested far-reaching reforms to the city's transport system, which included, remarkably, the total phasing-out of trolleybuses, which apparently offered no advantage over motor buses. One wonders whether said consultant had actually spent any time in the city's streets, absorbing the pungent diesel fumes emanating from the motor buses, as poorly maintained as the non-polluting trams and trolleys.

And so to San Francisco — California, the Promised Land, Home of the Beautiful People, etc, etc. Yes? Well … not quite. Alighting from our Chicago train at Oakland and delivered thence by bus across the Bay to our hotel just off Union Square, in the heart of the city, I was somewhat shocked to find as many beggars and down-and-outs as I had seen in Moscow and St Petersburg. I'd forgotten about Skid Row.

San Francisco shared other, less disturbing similarities with St Petersburg. Both have a splendid setting by the sea (or rather just a little inland from the open sea), that being the reason for their initial existence and for modern-day trade. Each possesses many fine buildings, and — now we're getting to the point — each operates large fleets of motor buses, trams *and* trolleybuses. In fact San Francisco has the largest trolleybus fleet — some 344 vehicles — in North America. And not only does it look after them, but it is constantly buying new ones and is planning various additions and extensions to the 17 routes currently operating. The oldest, 60 New Flyer 40ft-long bendi-trolleybuses, date from the early 1990s, whilst there are another 33 ETI Skoda articulated trolleys delivered in 2003. Most numerous are the standard four-wheel ETA Skodas delivered between 1999 and 2003; these seat 41 passengers with room for 40 standees. The newest, delivered in 2006/7, are 88 hybrid electric trolleys, 58 of them 40-footers, the rest 30-footers.

Below: A New Flyer articulated trolleybus in San Francisco in 2002. San Francisco Muni has the biggest trolleybus fleet in North America.

Although the USA led the way at the dawn of the streetcar era, and then again in the 1930s with its PCC cars, many of which were exported to Europe, modern San Francisco trolleybuses are built by Skoda in the Czech Republic. They are then shipped across the Atlantic and Pacific for further work, including fitting of much of the electrics and painting, which takes place in Maryland, and the finishing touches are carried out at Pier 15 in San Francisco.

St Petersburg is virtually flat, whilst San Francisco, as anyone who has ever watched a 'cops and robbers' chase filmed there knows, has some remarkable hills. There are, of course, the cable cars, which are really retained only as a tourist feature, but the trolleybus is ideally suited to ascending and descending the precipitous city streets, which afford wonderful views across the celebrated bay and its bridges.

San Francisco is a city that took global warming and the care of the environment seriously long before much of the rest of the USA, and electrically powered transport is high on its list of priorities. By the end of 2007 the entire SF Muni motor-bus fleet was operating on biodiesel. However, this was seen merely as one step forward. To quote a city official, 'SF trolleybuses are almost entirely pollution-free, since their electric power comes from the city's hydro-electric Hetch Hetchy Water & Power project … for many people the trolleybuses' quieter, cleaner service outweighs the unsightliness of the overhead wires.'

At the last count there were 359 trolleybus systems worldwide, operating a total of 2,523 routes, so whatever the future may hold in the UK there is plenty of interest out there beyond our shores.

A breath of fresh air

There was a time when open-top buses would be found only in seaside towns. The growth of leisure services has changed all that, as **Tony Wilson** discovers on a trip around Britain.

Right: During the 2000 summer season Lothian Region Transport operated this part-open-top Leyland Leopard on a service around Edinburgh's Holyrood Park and the volcanic outcrop of Arthur's Seat. Sadly, because of poor patronage, the service was not repeated in subsequent years. The vehicle had been new in 1977 to Western SMT.

Left: A more popular Edinburgh service was operated around the same time by Mac Tours. Then still a small independent company (it would later be acquired by Lothian Buses), it ran a variety of vintage buses, mainly double-deck, on a sightseeing service around the city. Unique in the fleet was this Leyland Tiger PS1, which had originally operated in the Channel Islands. Here, with a maximum load, the bus growls noisily as it pulls itself up and away from Waverley Bridge into Princes Street at the start of a mid-day tour in August 2001.

Right: At the eastern end of the Yorkshire Dales lies the tranquil town of Leyburn, where in the late 1990s moves were afoot to restore a passenger railway service under the auspices of the Wensleydale Railway Company. Prior to the start of rail operation the company ran a seasonal bus service at the eastern end of Wensleydale, one of the vehicles used being this ECW-bodied Bristol VR, seen departing Leyburn in July 2000.

Left: Few minibuses have served as open-toppers, but just such a vehicle was found during the late 1990s, operated by the Yorkshire-based T. J. Walsh company. Proclaiming itself to be 'Britain's Only Open-Top Minibus', it was a Ford Transit with Carlyle bodywork built in 1985 and is seen transporting customers around the delights of Halifax in 1997.

Right: Slightly larger — and definitely older — was this handsome Beadle-bodied AEC Regal. As the Kent registration suggests, the vehicle was new to Maidstone & District. It subsequently passed through various hands, and by the year 2000, when this photograph was taken, was in the ownership of the Guide Friday nationwide tourist operation. It is pictured in Bourton-on-the-Water whilst operating The Cotswold Tour.

Left: Stagecoach has for some years been the major operator in much of Cambridgeshire. Its Cambus subsidiary operated this Bristol FLF on a seasonal service that linked several leisure sites, including the Nene Valley Railway, with Peterborough city centre. It is seen in a sylvan setting near Water Orton.

Left: In recent years open-top operation in London has generally been left in the hands of a few companies that specialise in such operations. However, on the odd occasion open-toppers have appeared on the main route network, as demonstrated by this London Buses Leyland Titan in July 1993. Then allocated to the London Central fleet, it is seen pulling away from Marble Arch into Oxford Street on route 12 to Peckham.

Left: The 12m-long MCW Metroliner proved popular in later life as an open-topper because of its high top-deck seating capacity. Most were originally National Express coaches. Seen in a more sedate role in August 1996, an example in the London Coaches fleet heads along Tooley Street in a livery promoting the Tower of London, just across the River Thames.

Right: During the early 1990s Surrey County Council, along with the Surrey Hills Visitor Project, supported a number of leisure services that were grouped under the 'Surrey Hills Leisure Buses' name. This was a quite remarkable network and included circular route 448 based on the county town of Guildford. The additional appeal of this route was operation by London & Country with an open-top Weymann-bodied AEC Reliance, which had started life with Maidstone & District.

Left: Several open-top Bristol Lodekkas were operated by the Bristol Omnibus subsidiary of the National Bus Company. On a dull day in August 1978 one passes through the centre of Bath carrying three hardy souls on the upper deck.

Right: Also pictured on a sightseeing tour in Bath, in rather more seasonal weather, in August 1993, is this much older Bristol. By now the operator is Badgerline, the privatised successor to Bristol Omnibus in the city, and the tour was operated in association with Guide Friday. The 52-year-old Bristol K was run with a crew of three — driver, conductor (on the rear platform) and courier/guide (on the upper deck at the front).

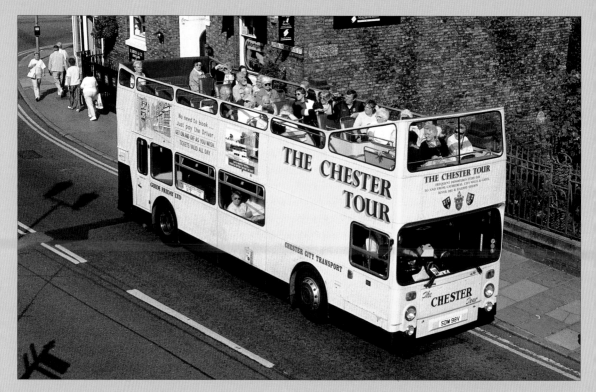

Above: Chester in the summer of 1995, by which time a couple of Chester City Transport's Northern Counties-bodied Leyland Fleetlines had been converted to open-top for use on a sightseeing tour. Making its way along Northgate towards the city centre, this one was photographed from the city walls at the Bridge of Sighs.

Below: In July 1997 a heritage tour of Liverpool was operated by this handsome Weymann-bodied Leyland PD2, which had been new to Southport Corporation. Here the bus, by now with Mersey Pride, waits at the revitalised Albert Dock.

Above: In 1998 open-top double-deckers could not be used in Manchester because of height restrictions necessitated by the overhead wires of the Metrolink tram system. To get around this, local operator Ashalls Coaches acquired a Leyland Leopard coach with modified Duple Dominant II body. The tour appears not to have been a great success, operating for only a short time. The coach had started life with Alexander (Midland).

Below: Of Britain's inland open-top services, one which ranks particularly highly is that operated in the Lake District by Stagecoach. In May 1995 this ex-Portsmouth Corporation Leyland Atlantean/MCW, in eye-catching Lakeland Experience livery, was photographed in Grasmere *en route* for Bowness-on-Windermere.

Only a number

Richard Walter approaches a milestone birthday and looks back at (almost) 50 years of bus enthusiasm.

All photographs by the author

I have approached 2008 with a certain dread and anticipation. In August I hit the big Five-O, much to the apparent amusement of my wife (40 last year) and my 10-year-old daughter and six-year-old son. I don't feel like 50 — but then, what is one supposed to feel like at 50?

So what is it about one's 50th birthday that makes it such a landmark? Well, rather than dwell on the age aspect, the receding grey hair, aching muscles, grumpy-old-man syndrome and the growing number of potions in the medicine cupboard, I thought it would be a good time to reflect on my first 50 years — or rather the period when I decided that I liked buses.

I am reliably informed by my parents that, even as a toddler in my push-chair, I was making gurgling noises at the shiny madder-and-white and green-and-cream buses that filled the streets of Edinburgh. My earliest favourite toys consisted of Dinky and Corgi model Routemasters and that oh-so-treasured Dinky Atlantean. As I look through my current collection of highly detailed CMNL, EFE and Corgi Omnibus mini-masterpieces, probably nothing captures the same feeling as owning that Dinky Atlantean, however primitive it might seem now.

Below: DMS-type Fleetlines were used by London Transport and other operators on sightseeing tours in the capital. In the summer of 1984 this Metro-Cammell-bodied bus, by now operated by Crouch End Coaches, was running on hire to its original owner in LT Sightseeing Tour livery.

This is an official London Sightseeing Bus.

OJD 222R

Above: In 1992 London Buses bought 40 Alexander-bodied Leyland Olympians. Operated by its Leaside Buses subsidiary, they ran mainly on route 253, as demonstrated by this smart example at Euston station.

As I ploughed through my education, two significant things happened. Firstly I joined the Bus & Rail Club at my school (Wow! There were actually other people who shared my obsession!), and secondly I was given my first camera — a very basic point-and-shoot which produced square prints. In those days it took about a week or so for films to be developed, and I remember well the anticipation of waiting for the results — shots of a battery-electric bus on loan to Edinburgh Corporation Transport, a broken-down Seddon midibus with mechanic in attendance, the real London Routemaster Dinky Toys overall advertising bus, to name but a few. Oh yes, the camera went on every family holiday from then on, and most of the pictures were local buses — Bristol REs and Lodekkas and the first Leyland Nationals.

I soon found I had developed a particular interest in all things Scottish (with a specific focus on my native Edinburgh) and in the London scene. For me there has always been something special about the London red bus — not just the iconic Routemasters but all the later vehicle types that were tried, many of which have come and gone in a twinkling of an eye.

As the years went by and I settled into a life-long employment in NHS administration, my cameras were upgraded and replaced — usually when they had been used so much that they literally fell to bits. Prints gave way to slides in the early 1980s, and I used Agfachrome film before switching in the mid-1980s to Kodachrome 64 film, which I stuck with for many years before progressing to Kodachrome 200. In more recent years I have moved to non-process-paid Kodak Elite Chrome 200, as sending films straight to Switzerland for developing (and indeed the USA now) became a laborious and unsatisfactory state of affairs. (Here you will note the grumpy-old-man syndrome creeping in.)

Over time my photographic techniques changed. Taking record shots of buses in town locations was fine, but I much preferred trying to capture them in more scenic and exotic settings. If this included standing in freezing-cold snow showers and gales then so be it — no-one said bus photography was easy.

Then there were the hours hanging around to picture a particular bus in glorious sunshine only for (a) that bus to have been changed over for a much less interesting vehicle, (b) the sun to disappear behind a minuscule cloud at the exact moment the camera shutter clicked, (c) a cyclist or passer-by to walk straight in front of the camera at the vital moment or, even more annoying, (d) another bus photographer to appear from nowhere and step right in the way. Oh, the joys …

Over the years I have made many 'bus friends', many of whom work within the industry. However, just as I have encountered many, many good-natured and helpful drivers, I have also fallen foul of a few. Some are suspicious of why photos are being taken (could I be a spy from Social Security?). Others don't appreciate that often the reflective glazing on modern buses doesn't show their faces clearly and don't want their pictures taken.

The number 50 has featured prominently in terms of bus-related activities. There was the 50th anniversary of London Transport, with that wonderful all-gold Routemaster. Then there were the Queen's Silver and Golden Jubilees, marked by the appearance up and down the country of buses in silver and gold liveries.

In the late 1980s something happened that changed my life totally. I met and fell for a girl from the Western Isles, and for the next few years my bus activities were to be restricted — well, you have to make a good impression, don't you? Going to Stornoway to meet the in-laws was pretty daunting, but the blow was lessened by the discovery of all the fascinating local bus fleets and the cast-offs from the mainland — many of which were former Scottish Bus Group vehicles.

Imagine my delight in finding that my mother-in-law had an attic with windows which allowed photos of the local bus service against a great scenic backdrop. I wouldn't say that swayed the decision to get married … but it may have helped.

Left: An Alexander-bodied Olympian of a rather different sort, although also in London and with a registration transferred from a Routemaster. The year is 2003, and the vehicle is on Stagecoach's new Megabus operation. It was one of a trio of three-axle Olympians purchased by Stagecoach in 1989.

Below: Wintry weather in Scotland's capital, and a Lothian Region Transport Alexander-bodied Atlantean braving the snow.

Above: Unusual buses in the Lothian fleet were 18 Leyland Cubs with Duple Dominant bus bodies, delivered in 1981. The Cub was derived from the Terrier truck chassis and built at Leyland's Bathgate plant.

Beside the inevitable changes over the last 50 years in vehicle design and specifications, we have seen other major changes in public transport.

First there was deregulation, which gave greater scope for interesting photos — more than any other time in recent years. In Scotland the Glasgow (and, to a certain extent, Edinburgh) bus wars were a fascinating moment in history. All of a sudden Routemasters were appearing in vast numbers in colourful liveries, while the term 'bread van' took on new meaning as fleets of minibuses arrived.

Then there was the development of the new big bus groups. From its early days at Walnut Grove, Perth, Stagecoach expanded not only its bus services but rail links worldwide, while First spread from Aberdeen waving its magic wand and turning many fleets into 'Barbies'. Arriva and Go-Ahead were not far behind. In my home city Lothian Region Transport survived the takeovers, and Lothian Buses has become a fine example of a progressive and successful company, losing its coach fleet along the way but gaining a hugely successful open-top tour network. Its harlequin-liveried low-floor bus fleet had by 2008 almost entirely replaced the traditional madder-and-white vehicles.

But probably the single biggest change in my hobby has been the introduction of digital photography.

The traditional equipment of the bus enthusiast has been replaced almost overnight — gone are the ring-bound notebook, pocket tape-recorder and supply of pencils and films, along with the shoulder-bag and the SLR and movie cameras. Now we have hi-tech gear complete with MP3 player (which records, categorises and prints out fleet lists) and an 8-megapixel digital pocket-size zoom camera with a 2-megabyte memory card which also takes video films. Perhaps the optional T-shirt and baseball cap haven't changed, but the new-era bus enthusiast is prepared for all eventualities.

The good thing about the arrival of digital is that almost anyone can now take a good photo. Pictures can be stored on picture discs and PC hard drives and can be edited and augmented to give the best possible result. I have had hours of pleasure scanning-in slides and removing unwanted shadows and lamp-posts that may have spoiled the original shot. Who would have thought it possible?

The downside is that traditionalists like me (and I do now own a digital camera too) are finding it more and more difficult to obtain slide films and, indeed, even to locate camera shops. The change has happened as predicted a good few years ago but has moved forward at a pace no-one could have imagined.

And what of my next 50 years? I am sure that they will see all sorts of interesting changes in the world of public transport, and, grumpiness and mobility allowing, I will still be capturing some of these on film, memory card or whatever other medium is around the corner.

Top: As deregulation loomed in the mid-1980s the Scottish Bus Group embarked on a marketing campaign based on the 'Best Bus' theme. An Eastern Scottish Leyland Olympian with ECW body at Arthur's Seat claims to be the 'Best Bus Around'.

Above: Even older than the author is this Leyland Tiger PS2 operated by Classique Coaches of Paisley. It dates from 1950 and has stylish bodywork by Harrington of Hove.

Right and below: A Volvo Olympian of Dublin Bus promotes baked beans, while north of the border a Translink Leyland Tiger offers tomato sauce. Both buses have bodywork built by Alexander (Belfast). The Olympian was new in 1997, the Tiger in 1991.

Right: Bus na Comhairle operates services from Stornoway, where the author has family connections. Its fleet includes this VDL SB200 with Plaxton Centro body, delivered in 2007. The romantic-sounding 'comhairle' translates into the rather prosaic English 'council'.

Backing the bus

In recent times more local authorities have seen the benefits of working with bus operators to improve services. David Thrower looks at how bus operation has changed over the years.

B us travel in Britain arguably started with John Greenwood's pioneering service in Salford in 1824 and George Shillibeer's service from Paddington to the Bank in London in 1829. But really the bus in its motorised form has been with us for only 100 years.

For the first two-thirds of that century, buses didn't really need that much help from outside the industry.

Bus companies went about their business in a very matter-of-fact sort of way. Staff were recruited, fleets expanded or renewed, garages enlarged or rebuilt, and from the middle part of the 20th century trams and, later, trolleybuses were replaced with motor buses. Most of this was achieved efficiently, quietly and without fuss, and without much help from outside.

By the 1930s faster, diesel buses had started to appear in common use, and dependable classic designs such as the Leyland Titan and the AEC Regent were giving bus travel a good name. Indeed, it's remarkable in retrospect to think that the gap between the horse bus and AEC's Renown six-wheeler of 1929 was a mere 20 years, and that the gap from the horse until London Transport's stunning 1939 RT design was only 30.

We didn't know it at the time, but the 1930s, the late 1940s and the early 1950s were to prove a golden age for bus travel. Demand was high, and congestion, although a factor, was eased in part by the virtual disappearance from the streets of the horse, car ownership still being low. Labour was still reasonably cheap, and reliable buses had been made far easier to drive through such inventions as the pre-selector gearbox and air braking. The bus was king of the road, and that was largely that.

Just occasionally Government had had to step in, for example to create the London Passenger Transport Board (in 1933) or set up the Traffic Commissioner system. But in the main the bus business was much like any other and was largely left to get on with it.

But, as we all know, drastic decline was just around the corner. That 1950s 'You've never had it so good' affluence, which boosted demand for travel, also went on to boost wage levels and, in turn, the demand for cars, whilst slum clearance took away the high-density urban settlements that had so strongly favoured public transport — think of those once-magnificent long radial

roads into Birmingham, Liverpool or Glasgow, lined by sooty terraced housing or blackened tenements, with a shop on every corner, and how they were replaced progressively with low-density New Town estates, leafy suburbs and twee cul-de-sacs that offered far leaner pickings for bus operators.

Some statistics illustrate all too clearly the nosedive in the bus's fortunes. In 1950 about 13,000,000,000 journeys were made in the UK by local buses, plus almost a further 2,000,000,000 by trolleybus, making 15,000,000,000. By 1970 local bus journeys had slumped to less than 9,000,000,000, and trolleybuses had all but vanished. By 1980 the remaining local bus journeys were down to just 6,000,000,000. The figure now is around 4,500,000,000 — a little over one third of the number in the 1950s.

If such decline had continued at this rate bus use would theoretically have completely disappeared by around now — a startling thought. And the trolleybus and the tram (Blackpool excepted) really *did* disappear.

But, although bus travel was originally conceived as a 19th-century business, today it is increasingly regarded as much more than that, being valued as a means of trying to curb congestion and making good-quality transport available to all (thus interestingly still fulfilling the literal meaning of the Latin word 'omnibus').

And so decline has been grabbed by the horns and wrestled with. The buses and their advocates have fought back. Gradually bus operators, transport planners, traffic engineers and Government have

Left: In the 1930s a new generation of diesel-engined buses helped revolutionise public transport. This AEC Regent, with lowbridge Roe body, was delivered to Baillie of Dumbarton in 1933 and is seen on the company's service to Glasgow, passing the Kelvin Hall. *AEC / Gavin Booth collection*

Right: In the 1950s bus use in Britain started its long decline, from a high of 13,000,000,000 passenger journeys a year at the start of the decade to 4,500,000,000 today. This is a Roberts-bodied Guy Arab in service with Darlington Corporation in the mid-1950s and in general design — front engine, 56-seat rear-entrance body — typifies vehicles operating at that time. *Gavin Booth collection*

worked more and more closely together to try to help the bus, much in the same way as environmentalists and ecologists have tried to save the tiger or the whale from threatened extinction.

Turning-point

Perhaps the most memorable turning-point nationally in the UK was the Bus & Coach Council's campaign of the early 1980s, with its catchy slogan, 'We'd all miss the bus'. This, for the first time, painted a stark picture of ever-worsening decline in bus travel and of the knock-on effects for all road users.

But, in truth, campaigning on behalf of the bus — and taking measures to help bus travellers — had already got underway in the 1970s. At first physical

progress was painfully slow, as London Transport and other major bus operators struggled to persuade their local authorities and the public at large that buses really did need their assistance, particularly to overcome the strangulating effects of congestion.

And, throughout the 1960s and '70s, some policies had actually further damaged bus travel. The industry itself, in its desperate search for economies, had repeatedly cut services and raised fares, deterring short-distance riders in particular. With hindsight it seems a suicidal strategy — a higher price for a poorer service. Who wanted to pay higher fares for a lower-frequency service with SMS Swifts in lieu of lower fares and a nice friendly conductor on higher-frequency RTs?

Left: One-man operation, initially of single-deckers, was adopted by a growing number of urban operators in the 1960s. In 1965 Grimsby-Cleethorpes Transport took delivery of a trio of AEC Reliances with 42-seat dual-door Willowbrook bodywork. Specifying two doors was common practice on urban one-man buses and, as this picture shows, allowed passengers to board while others were still alighting. *T. W. Moore*

Right: One-man operation had drawbacks for passengers, including the disappearance of the conductor. This conductor is on a Cumberland Motor Services Leyland Tiger in 1964. Ironically the vehicle is one which has been converted to operate as a one-man bus by the removal of much of the bulkhead behind the driver. *A. Moyes*

There developed a tangible hostility between bus operators and their customers, the former blaming the latter for not having the correct change for driver-only buses and for being slow and bumbling as they boarded, and the passengers blaming the operator for late-running services and miserable cattle-truck 'standee' vehicles.   And both operators and passengers blamed the manufacturers for unreliable buses — think of those AEC Swifts, for example, or Newcastle's Panthers. It wasn't a happy time. And it went on for several decades.

Fares were perhaps the greatest source of discontent amongst passengers. In the early 1980s local-bus fares headed for the then-astronomical £1 level, except in a few areas such as South Yorkshire, where massive subsidies were poured in until stopped by Central Government's unsympathetic intervention.

Traffic

Early traffic policies also seriously disadvantaged the bus, with inventions such as one-way systems that re-routed buses away from their stops in city centres and increased the distances they covered between successive road junctions, sending them around the back streets with all the other traffic.

Granted, traffic delays had ever been an impediment to bus travel in the big cities and the larger towns. Motor-bus services in cities such as London, Manchester, Newcastle upon Tyne and Glasgow had also been bedevilled in the golden age by electric trams stopping in the middle of the road to set down and pick up passengers, and by the slow speed of horse-drawn traffic. Even the dear old trolleybus had caused its own congestion at times. Meanwhile the number of private cars has soared,

Above: The first bus lanes were introduced in the 1960s, but 40 years on they can still be controversial. London, which pioneered their use in Britain, has an extensive network. A London General Volvo B7TL is seen in Charing Cross Road. *Stewart J. Brown*

A major step forward in thinking came in 1973 with the proposal for London's 'Speedbus' network. This was for limited-stop routes using a comprehensive system of bus lanes. But always there seemed to be resistance from the authorities that did not want to upset the motorist, and so the new thinking struggled to make headway. Bus lanes really needed to link up into a coherent network if they were to speed up the buses.

But almost no-one, other than a handful of academics and bus-industry spokesmen, stood up to the remorseless advance of the private car. In fact proponents of bus travel had a surprisingly hard time. In Manchester bus lanes were installed only to be burned off the road surface when there was a change of local government. A further change would see the bus lanes reinstated, and so it went on, the road-markings being painted on and then burned off in seemingly rapid succession. It has taken an entire generation of effort to make them stay for good.

Enforcement once the lanes were in was another matter. Again, London tried to lead the way with some catchy posters about drivers who parked illegally in bus lanes, causing traffic chaos ('He stopped for a paper. So did everybody else').

It was only when closed-circuit television equipment became sufficiently cheap and reliable, in the 1990s, that enforcement of bus lanes and bus-only streets became a practical proposition. There is nothing like the thought of a bus behind them filming them as they infringe local traffic-regulation orders, followed by an automatic fine through the post, to keep errant motorists out of buses' exclusive territory.

Bus stations

It also seems obvious that, to help the bus as a means of travel, we should have bus stations. But there has long been a debate about whether we really do need bus stations in this country. After all, inner London has very few, yet life goes on. But many people like to have a bus station, rather than a hotchpotch of stops and a string of sometimes tatty shelters in windy side streets.

And there are other advantages — bus crews can have a canteen, there can be provision for a café, a newsagent and toilets, as well as an office where passengers can obtain timetables and buy weekly passes, and it obviously makes sense to group these together. For a passenger who's new to a town, too, a bus station is a reassuring place.

But by the 1960s many of the bus stations that had been established in the 1920s and '30s were looking anything but inviting, exuding a greasiness and scrappiness that deterred passengers. Worse was to follow, some bus stations being entombed beneath shopping centres or multi-storey car parks in the planning-nightmare era of the 1970s.

from about 2 million in 1950/1 to about 27 million today, not to mention a further six million lorries and other vehicles. No wonder there seems to be so much traffic about.

The result in many areas has been to lower traffic speeds to that of the days of the Edwardian horse bus, making life extremely difficult both for bus operators and for passengers. After all, there is little point in urging motorists to travel by bus if those buses themselves are mired in the congestion caused by other motorists. The bus has needed help, and lots of it.

There was only limited sympathy for the need for bus lanes at first, and even some opposition from vested interests. I recall attending an early-1970s public meeting in Central London to debate the installation of the westbound bus lane in Piccadilly. Putting a bus lane in, so its opponents loftily argued, might get in the way of wealthy customers being dropped off by taxi at Fortnum & Mason's. Fortunately LT's supporters were equally vocal, and the bus lane went in (and is still there today).

Paris, it was pointed out at the time, already had 90 bus lanes, yet here was London agonising about adding just one. London gradually introduced more and more bus lanes — the first contra-flow bus lane being introduced on Tottenham High Road in 1970 — but it was to be slow going, and, although some other cities slowly followed suit, progress everywhere was patchy.

Above: Bus stations became a feature of many towns and cities from the 1920s. Durham's boasted a particularly fine frontage. The crew of a United Leyland Tiger pose for the photographer. *Gavin Booth collection*

Right: When opened in 1969 Preston's bus station was hailed by its designers, Building Design Partnership, as the largest in Europe. Featuring 80 departure bays and located under a multi-storey car park, it cost £1.1 million. Forty years later its future looks bleak, as there are plans to demolish it. The bus is a Preston Corporation Leyland Titan PD3. *Gavin Booth collection*

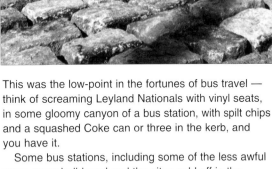

Below: Many 1970s bus stations were bleak, unwelcoming places, among them Anderston, in Glasgow. Opened in 1973, it closed 20 years later. Here a Central SMT Bristol Lodekka is seen leaving the newly opened terminal. *Stewart J. Brown*

This was the low-point in the fortunes of bus travel — think of screaming Leyland Nationals with vinyl seats, in some gloomy canyon of a bus station, with spilt chips and a squashed Coke can or three in the kerb, and you have it.

Some bus stations, including some of the less awful ones, were bulldozed and the sites sold off in the freebooting 1980s. There were some modest successes with new bus stations in PTE areas, such as Huddersfield and Bury Interchange, but just as many failures.

Today the bus station still isn't a universally admired concept. But we are now seeing some really first-rate bus stations being constructed — Warrington Interchange being an outstanding recent example — and, at long last, bus-station design is really beginning to assist bus travel rather than be provided as a downmarket feature with windswept aprons, smeary glass and unspeakable toilets.

Left: With peaked cap and clipboard, the inspector played a key role in keeping buses running, whatever the weather. Here in a sleet storm an Alexander (Midland) inspector briefs four drivers who are taking over buses being used on a vehicle-evaluation exercise, the vehicles in question being a Fleetline, a Metrobus, an Ailsa and a Dominator. A workshop supervisor looks on — perhaps with fingers crossed as he contemplates the challenges of running four different types. *Gavin Booth collection*

Keeping in touch

Another way of helping buses to run smoothly has been the development of communications systems. In the 1950s roadside inspectors had a peaked cap, a clipboard and a pencil, all designed to frighten the bus driver into running punctually. But there was little an inspector could do about late running, apart from keeping in touch by telephone with Control (if there was one) or the garage (if there wasn't) to feed back information on delays and to try to warn of any likely problems.

The first serious attempt to use technology to help the buses to run more smoothly was London's 'Bessy', actually BESI (Bus Electronic Scanning Indicator), an electronic roadside scanner that read a coded plate on the side of the bus, between-decks, and which kept track of where buses were, how well spaced they were and where any service gaps were developing. The first units were trialled in the 1950s, so this really was cutting-edge technology, quite far ahead of its time. The system was a little cumbersome, by today's micro-chip standards, but it did work.

In the 1970s radio control came in, drivers being able for the first time to communicate direct with a central control office. Although such inventions didn't actually get rid of the traffic jams — or make up for the chronic staff shortages — they did enable buses to be turned short of their final destinations where this would help the overall service in the interests of the majority of passengers. Subsequent advances in technology have made radio systems far more reliable and effective, and they are now an accepted part of bus operation.

Speeding up boarding

The catchy 'Hop on a bus' slogan owed its origins to a publicity campaign in London that tried, after the self-defeating seven-week 1958 bus strike, to restore patronage. But the process of 'hopping on' buses was itself made much more difficult by the trend during the 1960s and '70s towards one-person operation. The introduction of what at the time were one-man (rather than one-person) buses took place under the mid-1960s Labour Government of Harold Wilson, during the regime of its Secretary of State for Transport, Barbara Castle. To speed the process, operators purchasing new buses suitable for driver-only operation could reclaim from Government 25% of the cost (later increased to 50%).

The scheme was extremely successful, sending thousands of what were often regarded by the public as old-fashioned vehicles to the scrapyards. Effectively it spelled the end of the Bristol Ks and Lodekkas, the Leyland PD2s, the Crossleys and Guy Arabs and the AEC Regents of many fleets.

From the passenger's perspective the difficulties in paying a fare on boarding centred on two issues — that initial act of getting on board, which is always slower for those who are older, have small children (or shopping or luggage) or experience a disability, and the actual act of paying the fare.

It was to be several decades before paying fares became a swifter process than was initially the case. In the early days understanding complex fare structures, sorting decimal coinage, finding change for bus travel and handing it to a driver, who had to count it, set a decidedly cronky ticket machine and then issue a ticket, which then had to be picked up by the passenger before they moved on down the bus, all added up to excessive time. It compared unfavourably with the open-platform crew-operated bus, which passengers simply swarmed aboard, paying only once they'd sat down.

What was to be done? Providing self-service machines (or driver-worked equipment) and turnstiles caused all sorts of problems. Machines varied from bus fleet to bus fleet and were unreliable and puzzling to non-regulars. Everything was tried to solve the problem. Remember Johnson fareboxes? And Videmat? And Autoslot? Nothing seemed to work well.

In the end, after years of frustration for all concerned, the problem was eased by the use of much simpler fare tructures, which have speeded up boarding, but there's still much to be done. It may be that developments in electronic ticketing will dramatically ease future paying problems. In any event, many passengers now have passes of one sort or another, and older people don't pay at all, cutting out millions of transactions.

Deregulation

Bus deregulation was arguably the greatest single measure taken to assist bus travel. In many ways, and in many places, it didn't work, or at least didn't work very well. But it did represent an attempt to go back to first principles.

Below: Britain's first busway opened in Runcorn in 1972 and represented a quite remarkable achievement. The dual-door Seddon Pennine RU operated by Crosville was the last word in modernity when the busway opened. *Gavin Booth collection*

If bus operators want support from local authorities and central Government for, say, bus priorities — or other forms of support — they must take care to woo the voters in those areas with a vision of fleets of glossy high-tech vehicles. FirstGroup, having seriously annoyed the good residents of Manchester with its scruffy double-deckers, fortunately recognised this and went on to wow the citizens of York and Leeds, at least, with the stunning and futuristic 'ftr' articulated-bus concept.

Despite the teething troubles, the 'ftr' vehicles appear to have re-established the bus as king of the road, as such heralding a new and long-awaited dawn. Most passengers will yearn for other similar initiatives.

Future priorities

Over the next few years we will undoubtedly see the further spread of such aids as real-time information, and perhaps the development of further high-quality bus stations such as the recently built one already mentioned in Warrington and that in Eldon Square in Newcastle upon Tyne. Gradually the bus network will be made to feel more like a light-rail network, with information displays, better shelters and kerbs that match the height of the bus entrance.

The Fastway system in Crawley shows just what can be achieved, in this instance aided by limited guideway sections. Converting ordinary bus routes into 'bus rapid transit' is undoubtedly the most high-profile way of all of aiding the bus. In fact the concept was initially pioneered in the UK with the Runcorn busway, as long ago as 1972. Perhaps, at last, it is an idea whose time has come.

Above: There are now busways in a small number of towns in the UK, including Gravesend, where Arriva operates the 'Fastrack' service using Wright-bodied Volvo B7RLEs. *Gavin Booth*

Left: Edinburgh also has a guided busway, served by Wright-bodied Volvos fitted with lateral guidewheels that are linked to the steering. *Gavin Booth*

Above: Bristol is another city that is investing in buses and bus priorities. This bus lane provides fast access for a park-and-ride service operated by Wessex Connect using Volvo B7RLEs with Plaxton Centro bodies. *Stewart J. Brown*

Right: While local authorities provide improved infrastructure — bus lanes, termini — operators have played their part with route branding. One of the strongest advocates of route branding has been Go North East, which company's red-based livery has virtually disappeared, to be replaced by a multiplicity of local identities. This Wright-bodied Scania L94, seen in Gateshead, is a 'Fab Fifty Seven'. *Stewart J. Brown*

SBG survivors

Early in the 21st century a number of vehicles new to the Scottish Bus Group were still in service with its successors. **Billy Nicol** illustrates a selection.

Above: The standard 1980s double-decker for Midland Scottish was the unusual combination of MCW Metrobus chassis and Alexander R-type body. The 1986 deliveries were among the last to arrive with the standard SBG triangular destination layout, first seen in 1950 on AEC Regents for Scottish Omnibuses. Midland Scottish became part of First Edinburgh, which was still running this Metrobus in Falkirk at the start of the 2000s.

Left: At Eastern Scottish most double-deckers in the 1980s were supplied by Leyland. These included Alexander-bodied Olympians, among them this 1983 bus, still in service with successor First Edinburgh 20 years later.

Right: The mid-engined Leyland Lion, developed from a DAB chassis, was a rare beast. SBG bought 19 in 1986/7, of which 13 went to Eastern Scottish. First Edinburgh was still operating this example in 2004. Note that for some of its last Alexander R-type bodies SBG abandoned the triangular destination display.